OVER
40
AND
LOOKING
FOR
WORK?

OVER 40 AND LOOKING FOR WORK?

A GUIDE FOR THE UNEMPLOYED, UNDEREMPLOYED, AND UNHAPPILY EMPLOYED

Rebecca Jespersen Anthony
Gerald Roe

BOB ADAMS, INC.
PUBLISHERS
Holbrook, Massachusetts

Designed and illustrated by Rose Sheifer

ISBN: 1-55850-870-8

Published by
Bob Adams, Inc.
260 Center Street
Holbrook, Massachusetts 02343

A B C D E F G H I J

CONTENTS

Need a Job? Start Here

Employers hire the people who make the best overall impression. You don't have to be the best looking, the smartest, or the smoothest talker in town to get hired. It's more than luck, and there's no question that it's more than a matter of age.

PART I:
Real Problems . . . and Excuses

Who Am I? What Can I Do? A Crash Course

Think you don't have marketable skills? Chances are you do. Before you can sell yourself to an employer, you have to know what you can do, what makes you tick, and what turns you on and off. Don't skip this chapter—it's easier than it sounds.

And Age Isn't My Only Problem

Do you have so many problems that you don't know where to start? Don't throw in the towel yet. You can get past your obstacles (handicap, illness, criminal record, job hopping, poor work record, lack of recent experience) and build a future.

Underemployment:
Dead-end or Opportunity?

Unemployed? Underemployed? Unhappily employed? Feel trapped or degraded by your job? Letting your job define you, whether you are a banker or a bellhop, can be a disaster. Your job is what you do, not what you are.

NEED A JOB? START HERE

Unemployed. Underemployed. Unhappily employed.

You need a job—a new job, a different job, any job at all.

How do you find one? Who can help? Where do you start?

Wouldn't it be terrific if somebody just offered you a job and you didn't have to go through the headaches and hassles of trying to impress employers?

It could happen.

Or you could win the lottery and never have to work or worry.

Chances may be about the same.

 Luck can play a role in finding a job. If you're in the right place at the right time, a job can fall into your lap.

But if you're like most people, you can't depend on luck alone. If you want a job, you have to look for it.

Most good things in life take some thought, some time, some commitment. The right job is, for most of us, one of the good things. And finding it is well worth the energy and preparation required.

> *You don't have to be the best looking, the smartest, or the smoothest talker in town. But you do have to know how to make yourself look good to an employer. You must have a marketing strategy, a way to sell yourself.*

FOR SALE

For many people the idea of selling anything seems distasteful, if not impossible. Pushing a product makes us think of some forlorn little soul going door to door with a heavy sample case. Or a glib fast-talker pressuring the unsuspecting customer into a quick and possibly shady deal. These stereotypes are instantly recognizable; each of us has met or observed them.

But we have also encountered the highly competent, courteous, poised, and helpful salesperson who answers questions, gives information, and performs a genuine service. The effective salesperson can convince us of the merits of a product, help us see a need for it, and show us the benefits of purchasing it. That is exactly what you have to do in a job search. You must sell your product—and *the product is you.*

Who Me?

It's easy to find excuses. We all do it, usually to avoid feeling uncomfortable or unsure. And we don't have to look too hard; somewhere inside each of us is a little voice that can hold us back, that can make us question our abilities, our potential, even our worth.

People who are beginning to think about finding a job or changing jobs are among the most inventive at finding excuses to avoid the challenge of competition or the risk of rejection. Deep inside you, is there a little voice saying

✘ *I'm not as young as I used to be*

✘ *I don't look like a 20-year-old*

✘ *I don't have enough experience.*

✘ *I have too much experience*

✘ *I don't have a great work record*

✘ *I've been fired*

✘ *I've got too many strikes against me*

✘ *I don't know what to say*

✘ *I don't have a resume*

✘ *I don't make a good impression.*

✘ *I get too nervous in interviews*

✘ *I don't know what I want to do*

✘ *And I don't even know how much I'm worth*

No matter how long your list of excuses might be, no matter what your work history has been, *Over 40 and Looking for Work?* can help you overcome the rationalizations and cope with the real questions. If you've had one job, a series of jobs, even if you've never looked for a job before, this book will help you

understand what to do and when to do it,

correct past mistakes,

avoid trouble spots,

smooth out the rough spots,

get past your anxieties and insecurities,

realize that you, too, can be competitive,

and recognize that it's more than a matter of age.

A Matter of Age

Everybody knows employers won't hire older people. How often have you heard this statement? More important, how often have you said it yourself?

Looking for work is not easy at any age.

But let's get serious about the age factor. How does it affect your chances of getting a job? How do you see yourself?

Are You Feeling . . .

➤ *Sorry for yourself?*
Yes   No   Maybe

➤ *Unable to make the effort?*
Yes   No   Maybe

➤ *Afraid of new experiences?*
Yes   No   Maybe

➤ *Unable to learn new skills?*
Yes   No   Maybe

➤ *Unwilling to change your routine?*
Yes   No   Maybe

➤ *Dissatisfied with your appearance?*
Yes   No   Maybe

➤ *Overqualified?*
Yes   No   Maybe

➤ *Frightened of rejection?*
Yes   No   Maybe

➤ *Reluctant to meet new people?*
Yes   No   Maybe

➤ *Afraid of competition?*
Yes   No   Maybe

➤ *Insecure?*
Yes   No   Maybe

➤ *Reluctant to move?*
Yes   No   Maybe

➤ *Trapped?*
Yes   No   Maybe

L ook at the pattern of your responses. Most job seekers will have some responses in each category. If you have a majority of "Yes" checks, don't despair. Maybe you're just being honest. Do your "Yes" checks mean you're too old to get what you want?

Probably not.

How different would your responses have been at 17?

Every job seeker feels some insecurity, anxiety, or fear— it's not just a matter of age.

On the Brighter Side

Some of you may not feel a whole lot more secure now than you did at 17, but think about what you've done and what you've learned in the past 20 years or so.

Along with age comes experience, maturity, common sense, even wisdom. These qualities are exactly what employers are looking for. It's your responsibility to identify them and to present them convincingly to a potential employer.

Part 1

REAL PROBLEMS . . . and EXCUSES

WHO AM I? WHAT CAN I DO?

A CRASH COURSE

Some of you may remember the "let it all hang out" era and the various types of "Me" encounter groups aimed at self-exploration and self-realization. But you don't need a group to figure out what makes you tick. It's simply a matter of doing a quick self-analysis, a perceptions check.

This check is not difficult. And it shouldn't be intimidating. It's just a matter of putting the pieces together.

Self-knowledge is a part of the package you're putting together to help you succeed in getting a job. Before you can tell an employer who you are, you have to know yourself.

Word by Word

When you get the chance to describe yourself to an employer, don't count on submitting an autobiography. Employers don't have the time—or the interest—to read lengthy essays or to listen to long speeches about you. Instead of complex narratives, they want a few simple, clear, meaningful *words*.

Grab a pencil.

Cross out any words in the following list that *do not* describe you.

Do it quickly.

Don't ponder over any particular characteristic—your first reaction is probably accurate.

Don't worry about crossing out too many words (or too few). Just follow your impulses.

WORDS

able	curious	forceful
adventurous	daring	forthright
agreeable	dedicated	frank
alert	deliberate	friendly
ambitious	determined	gentle
amiable	dignified	gracious
analytic	diligent	gregarious
articulate	diplomatic	handy
bold	discreet	happy
businesslike	easygoing	hardworking
capable	effective	healthy
careful	efficient	helpful
cautious	elegant	honest
competent	energetic	honorable
competitive	ethical	humble
concerned	exacting	humorous
confident	fair	imaginative
cool	fast	incisive
creative	firm	independent
critical	flexible	influential

innovative	persuasive	successful
insightful	poised	supportive
intellectual	polished	tactful
intelligent	polite	talented
intense	political	talkative
intuitive	powerful	tasteful
kind	practical	teachable
knowledgeable	precise	temperate
literate	probing	tenacious
loyal	productive	thorough
masterful	punctual	thoughtful
meticulous	quick	tolerant
moderate	quiet	trainable
modest	reliable	trustworthy
moral	reserved	truthful
motivated	resourceful	unassuming
neat	responsible	unique
nurturing	responsive	urbane
observant	secure	verbal
open	sensible	vigorous
optimistic	sensitive	virtuous
orderly	serious	vivacious
organized	sharp	warm
outgoing	shrewd	willing
particular	sincere	wise
patient	stable	worthy
perceptive	steady	youthful
persistent	straightforward	zealous
personable	strong	

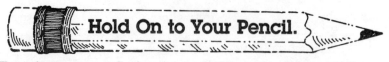

Hold On to Your Pencil.

There's one easy but extremely important thing left to do.

From the words that remain, choose no more than five

that give the best picture of you

—as you are,

not as you think you should be.

This can take some thought. Some of the words remaining on your list might be similar, or they may fall into groups. Try to choose words that give an overall view and that show the best picture of you.

WARNING

You might be tempted to skip this exercise and go right on to the next page.

DON'T DO IT.

If you don't do this exercise now, you'll probably never do it. Glossing over it will catch up with you when you reach the interview stage, if not before. Take the time to do it because other job seekers won't. Why risk being unprepared when you can so easily stack the deck in your favor?

These are five very important words.

They are the words you will use to describe yourself to potential employers.

Write them here:

1._____

2._____

3._____

4._____

5._____

and think a little more about yourself.
We all have some less desirable attributes as well.
But there is no need to advertise them or to
draw the employer's attention to them.
Honesty is important in a job search
but so is common sense.

Never Tell an Employer You Are

acquisitive

aimless

apathetic

arrogant

belligerent

boastful

bossy

brash

callous

careless

cold

combative

dictatorial

disruptive

dull

emotional

erratic

flippant

flirty

giggly

gossipy

hasty

haughty

impatient

impulsive

inconsiderate

insubordinate

irritable

juvenile

lax

lazy

lethargic

naive

negative

pessimistic

petty

pretentious

prying

rash

restless

slow

stubborn

suspicious

tardy

tearful

temperamental

vain

wasteful

weak

weary

willful

wishy-washy

Recognizing your faults or shortcomings is honorable. It can also be useful. Correct them if you can. If you can't, at least never allow them to surface in your contacts with potential employers. And once you're hired, keep these characteristics out of your working day.

Now Take a Break

Let's assume for a moment that you can have any job you choose, doing something you enjoy doing, something you look forward to doing each day.

Take a few minutes and daydream.
Picture yourself at work.
Imagine your job, your surroundings.
After a few minutes, open your eyes and ask yourself what you saw.
Were you

surrounded by people?	OR	working alone?
working with things?	OR	working with ideas?
putting things together?	OR	planning or designing something?
supervising others?	OR	being supervised?
taking orders?	OR	making decisions?
in a noisy, busy atmosphere?	OR	in a calm, relaxed environment?
exerting yourself physically?	OR	sitting behind a desk?
doing something repetitive?	OR	performing a variety of tasks?
competing with others?	OR	competing only with yourself?
feeling challenged, excited?	OR	enjoying working at your own pace?

Your imaginary job can tell you a great deal about your interests. Did your daydream give you a secure, comfortable feeling? If it did, you're probably on target, and you're at least halfway to knowing the kind of setting you'd like to work in and the kind of work you want to do.

If it didn't, dream on. . . .

This daydreaming technique is an effective way to narrow your job interests.

And all it costs you is a few minutes of your time.

Keep Finances Out of Your Daydream

There will be plenty of time to worry about money. Remember, this is not a commitment, just an exploration.

What Can I Do?

The next step in your self-analysis is to identify your skills.

Smart shoppers not only look for bargains, they read the label. The price tag can tell you only the cost; the label can tell you the value.

When you're buying a product—anything from a suit to a box of cereal—you check the label. You do this so that you know what you're buying, so that you don't get taken in by flashy packaging.

Employers, too, want to know what they're getting. They want to know as much as they can about the product—the job seeker—in order to avoid making a bad decision. Hiring the wrong person for a job is a costly mistake for an employer in both time and money.

Identifying your skills is like making a label for yourself. Just as you know what to expect from a shirt labeled "cotton," an employer will have expectations of you based on the labels you display.

For example, if your label says you have good writing skills, the employer can reasonably expect a sound knowledge of grammar, spelling, and punctuation and an ability to write coherent sentences and paragraphs.

Job seekers who can identify their skills and give them an appropriate label have a better chance of getting hired.

> *Regardless of what you've been doing, you do have skills to offer an employer. It doesn't matter if you've been unemployed, if you've been a home-maker, or if you've been trapped in a dead-end job—you still have market-able skills.*

This is a time for thinking positively. Excuses, negative thinking, and avoidance are sure to keep you where you are right now.

✘ *"I never learned any skills."*

✘ *"I don't know how to do anything employers are interested in."*

✘ *"I probably have some skills, but I don't know how to describe them."*

 These statements are cop-outs. If you never get past them, you'll be handicapped at every stage of your job search. If you don't identify your skills, how are you going to fill out an application form, especially one that asks what type of job you're applying for? How are you going to write a resume? How are you going to answer questions in an interview? How are you going to make a favorable impression on an employer?

You can get a head start at figuring out what you can do by rating your skills on the following chart.

Find the skills that apply to you. On the dotted lines, jot down some examples of how you used these skills in the past. It doesn't matter if you used them on the job, as a volunteer, or just for fun.

This is a very easy way to identify your skills and to develop some concrete examples to back up your claims.

Skills: What Am I Good At?

Rating—Be Honest!

	TERRIFIC	OK	LOUSY

Working with Hands

— — — — — — — — — —

Promoting Events or Ideas

— — — — — — — — — —

Finding Information

— — — — — — — — — —

Meeting the Public

— — — — — — — — — —

Following Instructions

— — — — — — — — — —

Working with Numbers

— — — — — — — — — —

Giving Instructions

— — — — — — — — — —

Caring for Children

— — — — — — — — — —

Understanding New Things

— — — — — — — — — —

Rating—Be Honest

TERRIFIC	OK	LOUSY

Selling Products

— — — — — — — — — —

Speaking in Public

— — — — — — — — — —

Delegating Responsibility

— — — — — — — — — —

Collecting Money

— — — — — — — — — —

Convincing Others

— — — — — — — — — —

Lifting Heavy Objects

— — — — — — — — — —

Meeting Deadlines

— — — — — — — — — —

Analyzing Information

— — — — — — — — — —

Using Computers

— — — — — — — — — —

Repairing Machines

— — — — — — — — — —

Rating—Be Honest

TERRIFIC	OK	LOUSY

Driving

– – – – – – – – – – – –

Investigating Problems

– – – – – – – – – – – –

Motivating Others

– – – – – – – – – – – –

Planning Meetings/Events/Agendas

– – – – – – – – – – – –

Listening

– – – – – – – – – – – –

Writing

– – – – – – – – – – – –

Editing

– – – – – – – – – – – –

Checking for Errors

– – – – – – – – – – – –

Handling Complaints

– – – – – – – – – – – –

Training Others

– – – – – – – – – – – –

Rating—Be Honest

	TERRIFIC	OK	LOUSY

Giving Information

— — — — — — — — — —

Budgeting

— — — — — — — — — —

Classifying Objects or Records

— — — — — — — — — —

Telephone Communications

— — — — — — — — — —

Typing

— — — — — — — — — —

Filing

— — — — — — — — — —

Advising Others

— — — — — — — — — —

Solving Problems

— — — — — — — — — —

Managing Time

— — — — — — — — — —

Showing Initiative

— — — — — — — — — —

Go back and look at your check marks. How do they compare to the ideal job you pictured in your daydream? If they are a close match, you're in great shape. You already know the kind of job you should be looking for. If there is an obvious mismatch, you've identified skills you need to acquire or refine. Either way, you are closer to realizing your goal.

The skills you rated "terrific" are the ones you'll want to draw to the employer's attention. Hide those you marked "lousy." And if you have time, work on your "OK" skills to improve them.

Once you figure out who you are and what you can do, the fun starts. Now you can begin to think about promoting yourself.

AND AGE ISN'T MY ONLY PROBLEM

What if you face other obstacles besides age? If any of the following conditions apply to you, keep reading. This section is for you.

➤ *physical handicap*

➤ *serious or chronic illness*

➤ *criminal record*

➤ *fired from previous job*

➤ *job hopping*

➤ *chronic unemployment*

➤ *no recent work experience*

Obstacles and Barriers

Let's talk frankly. Job seeking can be frustrating, disappointing, stressful, and intimidating even under the best of circumstances. Throw in a barrier or two, and the problems may seem insurmountable.

Yet finding a job is possible. Not necessarily easy but definitely possible. Keep in mind the many people who have found jobs in spite of personal and professional obstacles. Rather than being defeated by them, they have been able to recognize and overcome potential roadblocks.

Recognizing that there is a problem is the first step in overcoming it. The second step is learning to deal with the problem without apologies or excuses. Yes, it is easier for some than for others, but if you want to be employed, you will have to take a careful look at those things that may keep you from your goal.

Put yourself in the employer's position for a minute. Hiring a new worker is always a gamble. You want to reduce the risk as much as you can; you want to shift the odds in your favor.

Employers are good at spotting reasons not to hire. Often they don't let you know what's bothering them. That doesn't mean they haven't seen the problem. You have to be aware of your own barriers so that you can help the employer to see beyond them and get on to the real issue of your qualifications for the job.

Don't try to play hide-and-seek with the employer. Concealing a problem will only magnify it once it's discovered. Your ability to talk about your problem and to put it into perspective, showing how it has been resolved, is the key to receiving the same kind of consideration as any other applicant.

> *Patrick, an accountant, had had a problem with alcohol for fifteen years. He characterized five of those years as "a blur," during which he sometimes lived on unemployment, picked up odd jobs when he could, and drifted from one part of the country to another. Now he's been a recovering alcoholic for three years and has supported himself with a part-time job. He feels ready to get back to full-time work in his field. He recognizes his problem, he's no longer trying to hide it, and he is able to tell employers up-front why his work history looks the way it does.*

No employer is going to overlook the gaps in Patrick's career. If Patrick tried to pretend these gaps were of no consequence, he would be fooling only himself. His only chance is to anticipate the employer's questions and to get them out of the way as quickly as he can.

Don't Dwell on Your Problems

It doesn't matter whether you have had a long illness, a poor work record with several different employers, or a criminal record. Talk about the problem briefly, volunteer information the interviewer needs in order to see that the problem is not going to keep you from doing your job, and get on to the discussion of your skills and your abilities. If you don't, you won't get hired.

You may never be able to turn your obstacle into an asset, but at least you can deflect or minimize its negative impact. Know what you're going to say, anticipate the interviewer's anxieties or objections, and don't fudge on anything. If there's even the slightest hint that what you're saying is inaccurate or deceptive, the interview is as good as over.

Physical Handicap
Be ready to
▲ explain any special accommodations that might be required in your work station.
▲ talk about your condition in terms the interviewer will understand.
▲ illustrate successes or achievements in other jobs or in school to show that your condition does not prevent you from accomplishing the duties of the position.

Serious or Chronic Illness
Be ready to
▲ explain an interruption in your career.
▲ assure the employer that—at this point—your health will not cause problems with excessive absences.
▲ show by example that you have the stamina, the enthusiasm, and the ability to hold a job.

Criminal Record
Be ready to
▲ tell employers the nature of your conviction.
▲ discuss rehabilitation efforts.
▲ explain your current status (parole, halfway house, restrictions, etc.).

Fired from Previous Job
Be ready to
▲ tell the truth about previous employment.
▲ convince interviewer you have learned from past mistakes.
▲ communicate your desire and ability to hold a job.

Job Hopping
Be ready to
▲ explain circumstances of frequent job changes.
▲ assure the interviewer of your commitment.
▲ present a concise version of your employment history.

Chronic Unemployment
Be ready to
▲ state reasons for periods of unemployment.
▲ point out good work record on the job.
▲ demonstrate how your skills adapt to other jobs.

No Recent Work Experience
Be ready to
▲ show your awareness of current practices.
▲ talk about your reasons for re-entering the work force.
▲ exhibit enthusiasm and confidence.

Look Forward, Not Backward

Don't apologize.

Don't make excuses.

Don't try to justify.

Whatever has happened to you, whatever barriers there may be, don't spend your interview time rationalizing, justifying, or placing the blame on others. If you do, you might as well save your energy because you'll stay right where you are. Give yourself five minutes to talk about your barriers, how you have solved or are solving your problems, and then get on with those things that will help you get hired.

You may not have had any control over the things that have happened to you. You can control where you go from here. The biggest obstacle is a poor attitude. Get the chips off your shoulder; they're excess baggage, and you'll travel faster and farther without them.

Overqualified: Another Barrier

"Sorry, you're overqualified." That statement doesn't make much sense, does it? Have you ever met a teacher who was too good, a janitor who was too clean, or a surgeon who was too careful? How can you be over-qualified for the job you want? But some job seekers do hear this from employers.

What does it mean? Usually it refers to your education or your experience; the employer does not feel the job will meet your expectations or prove satisfying to some-one with your abilities or background. There may also be the feeling that your commitment will be only tempo-rary; as soon as you can find a position more stimulating, you'll be gone.

If you have a degree or two, or if you have had years of experience, your "qualifications" may, in fact, be a barrier in your job search. There's no easy way around it. Deception is not the answer—in one form or another, you will have to account for what you've done and where you've been.

One thing you can do is take a good close look at what you're saying and how you're coming off to be sure it really is the qualifications and not your attitude that's getting in the way. Watch out for these common traps:

☐ *Assuming that anyone should be happy to hire you because of your past accomplishments*

☐ *Coming off as arrogant, smug, or superior*

☐ *Dropping names and places to impress an employer*

☐ *Calling attention to college degrees if they're not required for the job*

☐ *Downplaying or ridiculing past accomplishments*

If you have a lot of qualifications, you may be rejected by some employers, and there's not much you can do about that. But you should also recognize at the beginning of your job search that "overqualification" can be a crutch for some employers. It's easier to say, "Sorry, you're overqualified," than it is to say, "Sorry, we liked someone else better."

UNDEREMPLOYMENT:
DEAD-END OR OPPORTUNITY?

The problem of under-employment exists in all occupations and affects workers of all ages and all levels of education. Most of us experience underemployment at some point in our working lives.

> *Larry Carter felt like a cog in a giant wheel. He did his job, but at the end of the day, he went home discouraged and unhappy. His duties presented no challenge and did not allow him to use the skills he had acquired in previous jobs. Because he knew he could handle more difficult responsibilities, he felt he was cheating both his employer and himself.*

Susan and Margaret are both executive secretaries in an insurance company. They are approximately the same age; each has worked for about twenty years and expects to work for twenty more. Both have acquired program debugging skills through training programs, but they are not using them in their present jobs.

Margaret is frustrated because she's using equipment she views as inefficient, slow, and outdated. She resents not having state-of-the-art equipment. She finds herself irritable on the job, she goes home angry, and she takes some of her frustrations out on her family.

Susan also recognizes that she is not using all her skills, but she does her work and makes the best of the situation. She doesn't dwell on what her job should be; she's content to produce as much as she can. She leaves the office at the end of each day without the tension and stress that Margaret carries home.

Both of these women are underemployed, but only one of them needs to do something about it. Margaret is a candidate for a hospital bed, a divorce court, or the unemployment line if this type of stress continues. Her health is at risk due to self-imposed stress, her relationships with her husband and family are at risk because of her negative attitude toward work, and her job is at risk because her discontent and stress affect the quality of her work.

Margaret has only two viable options in this situation: she can change jobs or she can change her expectations. Neither option is easy, but both are preferable to continuing in the same frustrating pattern.

Unlike Margaret, some people do not need great challenges, noteworthy accomplishments, or tangible rewards to make their jobs worthwhile.

You—or people you know—might work in order to

- *meet people*
- *keep busy*
- *have a place to go each day*
- *avoid boredom and stagnation*
- *escape from loneliness*
- *keep in touch with what's going on*
- *help others*
- *contribute to a cause*

At various points in their lives, people may actually prefer to be underemployed. High-paying, high-tech, and high-stress jobs are not for everyone. Some people choose a less demanding life style. Not everyone wants to take work home, go in early, stay late, put in extra hours on weekends, or be responsible for others' work.

Most people have to settle for something less than having it all. A demanding job may give you financial rewards but may not leave you with enough time or energy to be with family members, maintain a home, lend support to a spouse's career, volunteer for a favorite charity, pursue creative or leisure interests, or continue your education.

You may know of a few people who seem to have accomplished everything. What you may not see is the price tag. If you want a *career*, you will have to accept the challenges and responsibilities that lead to promotion and status. If you want a *job*, whether to meet your financial or psychological needs, that's OK too. Make the decision that is best for you.

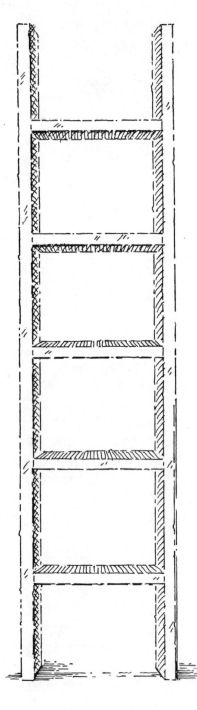

Underemployment as a Stepping Stone

Any job can be a stepping stone to better things. Even a job that is completely unrelated to what you want to do can demonstrate that you are employable. Just as you build a credit rating by using credit wisely and repaying your obligations promptly, you can build an employment history that helps potential employers see you as a good risk.

You've heard dozens of rags-to-riches stories. We know a man who started as a mechanic in a little shop in an alley in a midwestern town and today is an airline pilot for the biggest carrier in the U.S. Everyone has heard of the clerk who started at the bottom and built a corner store into a giant chain and a personal fortune. The list of personal success stories could go on and on. But they all have something in common.

> ***E**ach person who
> reaches the top builds
> on previous successes.
> And they learn from their
> mistakes. They're not
> perfect—they weren't
> necessarily born smarter,
> better looking, or richer.
> Some have quit bad jobs.
> Some have even been
> fired. But all of them
> have profited from their
> experiences.*

Are these outstanding successes luckier than the average person? Not necessarily, though luck can be a factor. Most people who are called lucky see an opportunity and pounce on it. Although it may often look like luck, success is probably a matter of timing, perception, assertiveness, daring, and a lot of hard work. Winning a lottery is luck. Using a job as a stepping stone is just good common sense.

Look, Learn, & Listen

You can use a job to learn new skills. Any job—from sweeping a floor to supervising a billion-dollar road project—affords opportunities to acquire or refine skills. Regardless of how low the level of the job or how poor the pay might be, there is always something to be learned.

Maybe your job teaches you a skill. Or maybe it doesn't ask you to do anything you haven't known how to do since you were 10 years old. That doesn't matter. You can always learn other things. Look around you. Watch other people. Listen to them. Pay special attention to your supervisor or to someone who has the kind of job you think you'd like. If you keep your eyes and ears open, you will

✓ *learn management techniques,*

✓ *learn how organizations work,*

✓ *listen to how people communicate,*

✓ *see how other people do their jobs,*

✓ *and, maybe, find out how they got there.*

What you're doing is preparing yourself for a better job.

Promotion. Some businesses have a tradition or policy of promoting from within. They may even have an un-written rule that everyone starts at the bottom. Regardless of your academic background or previous work experiences, you will start where everyone else did. In some organizations, promotions can come rapidly; in others, moving up to the next level may typically take several years. In any event, promotions usually go to people who do a good job at their current level of employment.

Let's say you've got an entry-level job and you recognize early that it can lead to bigger and better things. Whether it does depends on you and your goals. Once you master the routine, once you know your job inside and out, you can observe the work and the behavior of the people at the level above you. Be ready to step in if there's an opportunity for promotion.

It Is Not Possible to Move Ahead If You Think Your Present Job Is Beneath You and Does Not Deserve Your Full Attention and Effort.

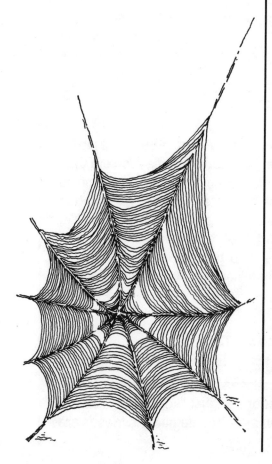

Dead-end Jobs

Don't ever let anyone tell you there aren't any dead-end jobs. There are. In fact, there are plenty of them. They are not restricted to factories, fast-food restaurants, and small businesses. They can be found in high-tech industries, giant corporations, and even in Fortune 500 companies. And it's not just the high-school dropout who's hired for a dead-end job. College graduates and even people with advanced degrees and years of productive experience can find themselves in jobs that don't lead anywhere.

Dangers of Dead-end Jobs

If you recognize that you are in a dead-end job, there are four dangers to be aware of and to avoid before the job becomes a trap.

1. Staying too long

Stagnation occurs when you know the routines of the job so well you no longer feel any challenge or excitement about performing the tasks. You settle back, do what you have to do, and tell yourself it's not the best job in the world, but it is a job, no one's bugging me, and I can put in my time, take home my check, and stay right where I am until I retire or drop dead.

2. Declining motivation

This is similar to stagnation but even more paralyzing. You put off or neglect duties, make excuses, and take no initiative to complete even your own tasks, let alone anyone else's. Don't be fooled into thinking you can cover up declining motivation. Usually, other people will be aware of it before you are.

3. Burnout

Again, this can only occur once you've been on the job for a while. Burnout, however, is even more of a problem than stagnation or declining motivation because you come to dislike, resent, even to hate the tasks you are expected to perform. You can't look at another patient, read another file, call another client, write another ad, or serve another meal. You've done it all before. You become impatient, crusty, irritable, or just downright miserable. Burnout can lead to severe depression.

4. Loss of self-esteem

This is the biggest danger. Burnout is job-related, but erosion of self-esteem touches every aspect of your life. The home situation deteriorates, just like the job. You are not the only one to be hurt by it. Your family and friends are also affected.

Some jobs become dead-end jobs not because of the nature of the work and not because the employer sees them that way but because you do. The main culprit for this is easily identified: it's called attitude. You feel sorry for yourself. You feel underpaid and undervalued. You let your attitude affect your performance on the job and sometimes off the job. When somebody asks you what you do for a living, you feel embarrassed or you evade the issue. Or you lie. You've taken the fatal step of letting your job define you.

You may dislike your job, but that is no reason to dislike yourself for doing it.

Moving On

If your present job does not meet your needs, allow you to use or expand your skills, or offer promise of promotion, don't conclude that the job is without value. Employers usually prefer to hire someone already employed than to take a chance on someone who cannot demonstrate the ability to hold a job.

The recommendation you receive for performing well can help you move on. While you are looking for new opportunities, you are earning money, occupying your time, and maintaining your image as a responsible, reliable worker.

TRAINING AND RETRAINING:

SHOULD I GO BACK TO SCHOOL?

Some people think that in order to get a job or to get a better job, they have to retrain, retool, or reschool. For those who are prone to make excuses for their employment problems, this is a good one.

Degrees, diplomas, and certificates are usually assets in a job search, but they are not always the answer. Concentrating on the skills, talents, and experiences you already have may be all that is needed.

Don't hesitate to take a course or two if it will give you additional knowledge or refresh existing skills, but be cautious of investing time, money, and energy in a training program that may not help in the long run.

> D on't use retraining as a substitute for action or as a delaying tactic.

Sure, if you decide you want to be a doctor, a lawyer, a dental hygienist, or a hairdresser, you have to be eligible for the appropriate license. And that probably means extensive training or retraining. If you need to go back to school to prepare for a new field and you're over 40, don't delay. Procrastination doesn't make the decision easier, and you're not going to get any younger.

Be a smart consumer. Before you commit yourself to a new program that will require a year or more of your life, get some answers to these questions.

- *How long will it take?*
- *How much will it cost?*
- *What are the opportunities in the field?*
- *Where are the jobs?*
- *How successful have recent graduates been?*
- *How much can I expect to earn?*

Don't be afraid to ask. Ignoring these questions can lead to disappointment and debt. If you buy a used car without inquiring about its background—or a new car without checking the price or the warranty—you could be stuck with a lemon. The same thing can happen with a training program.

A single class may be all that is required to enhance qualifications for any number of jobs. For example, an introductory computer class can familiarize you with terms and allow you to understand the basic operating procedures of information systems. Even one course in public speaking can increase your confidence and your ability to communicate with others.

How job specific does the training have to be? That's up to you. You can profit from any type of course. Suppose you take a class in cake decorating. That doesn't mean you have to look for a job in a bakery. What you learn about design, color, and balance can easily apply to many other fields. Also, you learn to plan, organize, and project costs. Many types of jobs will allow you to use those skills.

If you haven't been employed recently or if you've been stuck in the same job for longer than you'd like, taking even a single class can help clean out some of the cobwebs and give you a fresh outlook. Also, a recent course could enhance your resume and provide an interesting topic during an interview.

Whether you take one class or enter a formal degree program, additional education or training can help you

✓ *meet new people*

✓ *make new contacts*

✓ *increase your awareness*

✓ *gain self-confidence*

✓ *explore new areas of interest*

✓ *discover new career paths*

Classrooms Are All Around You

You don't have to be 18 to take advantage of a college campus. Most colleges offer a surprising array of educational opportunities, including noncredit courses meeting evenings or weekends, as well as semester-long credit courses. Walk on any college campus today—it's filled with nontraditional students, those who are older than the typical 18-to-22-year-old college student. More and more people are discovering it's never too late to learn.

Check out community colleges, vocational-technical schools, and proprietary schools. You'll be seeing more and more telecommunications courses, educational-television credit courses, and computer linkups for courses offered by a college or community college.

Enrolling in a college course to update your skills or to explore new interests is one option, but look around for others. Your community offers all sorts of interesting possibilities.

You won't have to look very far or very long to find opportunities to learn new things. Your public library might be a good place to start. They have more than books. Ask about courses offered in your community. Check with your local high school or community center to see what programs are offered for adults. Another possibility is the County Extension Office.

Don't ignore the "Instruction" section of your local newspaper's classified ads. You'll find ads for courses or seminars on many topics offered by individuals, groups, or even private businesses.

> You can better yourself at bargain prices. You'll be amazed at how inexpensive some of these courses are.

People go back to school for many reasons. Some take courses to prepare themselves for jobs; others simply take classes for enjoyment. Personal fulfillment is a worthy goal, and if you have the time and the money to pursue your interests, by all means do so. But remember, your goal is to get a job. If you're unemployed, underemployed, or unhappily employed, make your courses count.

Don't sit and wait for the twenty-first century to come to you. If the only thing you can do is turn on the TV set, you may have big problems competing for jobs in the years ahead. As a result of technology and global economic influences, the workplace is going to be different.

Becoming aware or keeping abreast of changes that will affect the nature of the work you want to do, learning new skills, and accepting the role of new technology will make the difference in whether or not you are employed. Don't pass up your chances to be a part of the work force.

Part II

OPENING DOORS

UNCOVERING JOB SOURCES

There are jobs available. No matter where you live, no matter what your previous experience has been, no matter how old you are, there is a job market. Knowing what's available to help you uncover job leads can make your job search shorter, less frightening or frustrating, and more productive.

The Silver Platter Syndrome.

Waiting for a job to find you could take a lifetime. Sure, it can happen. But it usually is the result of something you have done, something you have participated in, or something you have achieved. You can establish a reputation that others will remember and that will make them recruit you. But let's face it. Most of us find jobs by using conventional methods, such as advertisements, contacts and networking, employment agencies, or simply pounding the pavement and knocking on doors.

When Mary Hagedorn moved to a new city, she needed to find a job quickly. Unfamiliar with the community, she did not have family or friends to fall back on, nor did she have a network of contacts. The cheapest, fastest, and easiest method of looking for a job was to consult the classified ads in the city newspaper.

Successful job seekers have used all of the following methods—want ads, help-wanted signs, employment agencies, temporary job agencies, personal visits, and networking—at one time or another, often in combination. No one source is necessarily better, and no single source has greater status or offers greater chances for success. The methods you use will depend upon your qualifications, the amount of time you have, your financial situation, and your initiative.

Newspapers

Never overlook the obvious. All major newspapers carry a classified ads section, and thousands of jobs are advertised in daily and Sunday papers. You could spend hours reading through these ads, but your time will be better spent if you pick out those sections that fit your skills. Typical classifications include

Professional

Clerical

Technical

Sales

Medical

General

Domestic

Some of the ads look like a garbled mass of abbreviations. Space in the classifieds is expensive, and employers typically abbreviate common terms. Before you contact the employer, you need to know what they're talking about. This list of common abbreviations might be useful for a quick review.

Ad Abbreviations

account	acct.
accounting	acctg.
administrative, administrator	admin.
apartment manager	apt. mgr.
appointment	appt.
as soon as possible	ASAP
assist, assistant	asst.
available	avail.
background	bkgd.
bookkeeper	bkpr.
building	bldg.
calculator	calc.
cathode ray tube	CRT
certificate	cert.
clerk	clk.
college graduate	coll. grad.
computer	comp.
construction	const.
coordinate, coordinator	coord.
department	dept.
diploma	dip.
driver's license	dr. lic.
education	educ.
equipment	equip.
evening	eve.
excellent	exc.
executive	exec.
experience	exp.
full-time	f.t., FT
good	gd.
graduate	grad.
high-school graduate	hs. grad., HS grad.
hour	hr.
hourly	hrly.
housekeeper	hskpr.

license, licensed	lic.
manager	mgr.
maximum	max.
minimum	min.
Monday through Friday	M–F
month	mo.
necessary	nec.
need	nd.
operate, operator	oper.
part-time	p.t., PT
permanent	perm.
phone	ph.
possible	poss.
prefer, preferred	pref.
professional	prof.
reference	ref.
representative	rep.
require, required	req.
responsible	resp.
salary	sal.
secretary	sec'y.
supervise	supv.
supervisor	supvr.
technical, technician	tech.
telephone	tel.
telephone switchboard	PBX
temporary	temp.
ten-key adding machine	10-key
thousand	K (as $10,000 =$10K)
train	trn.
type, typing	typ.
week, work	wk.
weekly	wkly.
with	w/
words per minute	w.p.m., wpm
year	yr.

Help-Wanted Signs

Whether you live in a small town or a major metropolitan area, watch for window signs. They are inexpensive, easy, and effective ways for businesses to advertise jobs. Don't just walk on by, and don't assume that the jobs are only for teen-agers.

HELP WANTED

INQUIRE WITHIN

Employment Agencies

To provide assistance to job seekers and employers, each state operates a free job service. If you've never used one before, you can locate your nearest state employment agency by looking in the government section of your telephone book.

Private employment agencies can be found in most larger communities. These agencies receive job listings from employers and refer job seekers for specific positions. Private agencies charge a fee for their services. The fee may be paid by the employer, but don't assume this is the case. You may have to pay a commission (usually a percentage of your salary) to the agency if they help you find a job.

EMPLOYMENT AGENCY

Don't buy more than you need. Some agencies offer job counseling, resume assistance, and interview training. Be sure you need the services you buy.

Read the fine print carefully, and understand your obligations before you commit yourself to an agency.

Both public and private agencies may ask you to take aptitude, personal inventory, or skills tests. Don't panic. Relax and answer honestly. Bluffing is quickly spotted, and second-guessing almost always lowers your score.

TEMPORARY JOBS

Temporary Employment Agencies

If you want flexibility but you need some income too, an agency specializing in temporary assignments might be a good starting point. Jobs can include clerical work, typing, computer applications, maintenance, or factory work. You might work a single day, a week, or even a month or more. If you haven't been in the work force for a while, temporary jobs can give you a work record and recent references. They may even lead to a chance for long-term employment.

Personal Visits

Large businesses usually have jobs available at any time of the year. Your best chance of being considered for a position is to take the initiative to visit the personnel office. Most employers will accept unsolicited applications. You might find yourself in the right place at just the right time. On any visit to an employer, dress as if you were going to a prearranged interview. Always take your calling card—your resume.

Networking

"It's not what you know, but who you know." This tired old cliché remains a fact, and it is equally true in the upper levels of employment as it is in entry-level positions. It is possible to find a job without knowing a soul—people do it every day. But not all jobs are advertised. Many people hear about jobs through the grapevine. So it is often easier to get a job if you have developed a network of contacts who can help you.

The concept of networking is as old as the human race. In our everyday life we network all the time. We rely on people we know to give us information about and assistance in practically everything under the sun, from asking neighbors who painted their houses to asking the family physician to recommend a specialist.

Although we are all familiar with networking, when we apply the term to looking for a job, it sometimes seems to get blown out of proportion. A few years ago, *network* became a verb and also a hot topic on the lecture circuit. Suddenly the natural activity of gathering information from other people became mysterious, complicated, and difficult.

> *Networking doesn't require enormous sophistication or political maneuvering. It can and should be straightforward.*

Start by telling people you're looking for work. If you keep your plans a secret, nobody can help you. At first you may feel a little uncomfortable. Some hesitate because they are embarrassed about needing a job. Others are reluctant to admit they've lost a job. Let's face it: being out of work can hurt. But the situation could get worse if you don't ask for help.

Don't be confused about the purpose of networking. You're not asking for a job. You're not asking people to commit hours of their time to go out and pound the pavement for you. You're simply asking them to keep you in mind and to let you know if they hear of something.

If you approach people in the right way, you'll be surprised how helpful they can be. Most of us like to help when we can. And most of us are flattered by being consulted.

When you ask someone to help you—to become part of your network—tell them what they need to know. You might even give them a copy of your resume. But stop there. Don't make the mistake of telling them more than they need to know. Sob stories, tales of family crises, hard-luck tales, or tirades about the unreasonableness of your present or previous employer can only work against you. They can unwittingly be passed on to a potential employer.

Give It Time

Don't expect to build a network overnight. Like most useful things, it can take weeks—or even months. Not everyone you approach will be able to help, but perhaps they know someone who can. It's a very simple but direct referral system. It's much easier to call a total stranger if you can say, "John Jones suggested I call you."

Networks can help even without your solicitation.

George, your supervisor, has coffee with Charlie, who is in a similar position at another shop. It's not unusual for them to talk about their work, and Charlie happens to mention that he needs an ambitious, flexible person to take telephone orders. Although George doesn't want to lose you, he knows you have worked hard and deserve a promotion. He also knows that unless something unexpected should happen, he's not going to be able to offer you a better job. He mentions your name to Charlie, and when he gets back from coffee he tells you about it.

Does this mean you're going to get a new job? No! Now it's up to you. You take the initiative to call Charlie, introduce yourself, mention George's name, and ask when you can get together to talk about the job. There's no guarantee that George's recommendation will influence Charlie to hire you, but it will usually ensure that Charlie will talk to you. The rest of the selling job is up to you.

This is an example of how networking operates and how contacts can be instrumental in helping you work your way up. Such contacts are usually spontaneous, often arising in casual or social situations, and often they are no more than a way for you to get your foot in the door.

How Important Are Networks?

Networks are very important and very helpful. But they have to be used wisely. You don't depend on a network for everything. Don't waste time trying to put together a network for things you can do on your own. If you know about a job, go after it. Linda didn't, and she regrets it.

> *Linda Munoz saw a job at XYZ Company advertised in the daily paper. She knew her friend's uncle was a supervisor at XYZ, so she thought it would be a good idea to talk to him before she applied. She called her friend and asked for the uncle's phone number. He was out of town, and two days went by before Linda was able to reach him. During that time, someone else was hired.*

In this case, no middleman was needed. Trying to use a network caused delay and a missed opportunity.

Uncovering the Hidden Job Market

Because only 20 to 25 percent of all job openings are publicly advertised, networks can be very helpful for learning about the majority of available jobs. The hidden job market is no myth; it does exist, and there are some good reasons for it. To advertise a job opening costs money and requires hours of processing applications. Many employers have had good luck with referrals and prefer to hire individuals who have already received a good recommendation. If they're not required to advertise available positions and they feel fairly certain they can use the grapevine to fill the job, most won't use the newspaper.

Knowing someone—or knowing someone who knows someone—is the only way to find out about these jobs.

A contact can help you get an interview. Don't overwork it. Use your contact's name as an introduction, but don't continue to drop the name throughout the interview. Keep the emphasis on you.

Make New Contacts, But Keep the Old

Networking doesn't end when you land a job. Once you're hired, you have the opportunity to expand your network. New contacts can help you to learn the ropes and do a good job. They can even help you to move up either within the organization or in another.

And, of course, don't forget the networking that got you where you are. Good contacts, like good friends, should never be forgotten.

Network Notes

•• *If you don't have friends in high places, don't worry.*
They're not always the best sources for jobs, anyway.

•• *Don't expect too much.*
Networking contacts won't produce a job; they can produce a lead.

•• *Never beg or tell how desperate you are.*
Don't hurt your chances by pleading. Desperation is no substitute for qualifications.

•• *Don't be vague.*
Give your contacts the details they need to help you find a job. Saying "oh, anything will be fine" is not productive.

•• *Don't bug them.*
Get back to your contacts only when there has been a new development or you have something to report.

•• *Follow up on leads.*
Don't ignore any lead given you by a contact.
It only takes one.

•• *Don't depend on networks for everything.*
Networking is only one component of a job search; there are other ways of finding jobs.

•• *Networks can start anywhere.*
Don't overlook anyone; a person doesn't have to be rich or famous to be helpful.

•• *Don't forget a thank-you.*
When someone has been helpful, let them know you appreciate their efforts. You might need them again.

PROMOTING YOUR PRODUCT BY TELEPHONE

Telephones are an indispensable part of our daily lives. They are convenient, accessible, and easy to use. They are also annoying, time-consuming, and anxiety-provoking. Waiting for the phone to ring or picking it up only to hear an anonymous voice trying to sell a magazine subscription, aluminum siding, or lawn care services can bring out the worst in us.

Boycotting the telephone isn't the answer.

Look at the classified ads in your newspaper. How many of them list a telephone number? You'll find a high percentage do. Employers often list a phone number because they don't want to read letters, they don't have time to wait for applications to arrive in the mail, and they may want to do some preliminary screening quickly, easily, and relatively painlessly.

You might be one of those people who hates the telephone. You might even suffer from "telephone terror," a syndrome that leads people to babble, stammer, or freeze up.

Telephone terror usually occurs when you're caught off guard, when you're not organized, and when you don't know what to expect. It's not unlike a dating game. Whether you're making or receiving the call, there's always an element of uncertainty and the possibility of rejection. Some people are so traumatized by telephone anxieties that they avoid calls altogether. Well, there are other ways to meet people. But in a job search, the telephone is a tool you can't afford to dismiss or deny.

Your ☎ Is Your Friend

For job seekers, the telephone can be a valuable ally. This marvel of technology can make it possible to conduct an efficient, organized, productive, and inexpensive job search. As with any tool, to be most effective, it must be used correctly.

You can use the telephone to

1. gather information

2. inquire about available jobs

3. request application forms

4. arrange interviews.

THE MOST TYPICAL USE OF THE TELEPHONE IS TO ARRANGE AN INTERVIEW, AND THIS CALL CAN BE INITIATED BY THE APPLICANT OR BY THE EMPLOYER.

Know What to Say

Calling can be much easier if you have worked out your end of the conversation in advance. Just as business letters differ from personal letters, business calls are different from personal chats. They're a little more formal, a little more structured, and they have a clearly defined purpose.

For example, if you're calling in response to an ad in the newspaper, your conversation might start like this:

> **Hello. I'm Sidney Sample. I'm calling in response to the ad for a sales clerk in today's Chicago Tribune.**
>
> Pause here. Chances are the person on the other end will ask a question, make a statement, or transfer your call.
> If Nothing Happens, you go on.
>
> **I would like to arrange an interview for this position.**

Have your calendar handy. Know when you are available, and be ready to make a commitment. You may be given specific times and dates, or you might be asked when you could come in. Don't hem and haw, don't be tentative, and never ever say, "Oh, any time is fine with me."

And once the appointment is made, don't even think about calling back and asking to have it changed unless you come down with mumps or your house is on fire.

Before you hang up the phone, be sure you know

✓ *where to go*

✓ *whom you will see (the interviewer's name)*

✓ *the exact time to report.*

Then conclude quickly, with something like this:

Thank you. I look forward to seeing you.

Thousands of applicants lose out on jobs because they don't know how to use the telephone to their advantage. Remember that the purpose of your phone call is only to set up an interview. Don't try to sell yourself as a disembodied voice; your chances are much better in person than on the telephone. Many employers use the telephone to screen applicants; you don't want to be weeded out before you have a chance to show up.

TELEPHONE IMAGE

Suggestion: If you are asked about your background and qualifications, you'll find it much easier to give quick and accurate responses if you have your resume next to the phone.

Another good suggestion: Watch what you say–literally. Keep a mirror by your telephone. Watching yourself in a mirror while you are speaking on the phone can make you sound like a different person. If you pay some attention to your image, you'll find yourself smiling more, and this will carry over into your voice. You'll sound more confident, poised, and enthusiastic. It may sound silly, but it works. Try it.

> **You'll be a better job seeker if you follow these suggestions.**

TELEPHONE TIPS

Be Prepared
Have a supply of paper close at hand—and a pen that works!

Speak in a Pleasant Voice
Try to sound friendly, alert, and calm.

Cut Out Background Noise
Blaring radios, barking dogs, or screaming children are distracting for you and the person you're speaking to.

Train Family Members to Receive Calls
Be sure they know how to take messages, including the caller's full name and telephone number.

Use Interview Language
Think skills, attributes, and positive impressions.

Think about Timing
In response to an ad, call as quickly as you can. If you're making a cold call to inquire about possible jobs, you probably shouldn't call as soon as the employer's door is unlocked.

Smile!
It can't be seen, but your smile will help you sound relaxed and enthusiastic.

Don't Call Collect
You can call anywhere in the world for a few dollars. Even if the employer has authorized you to make a collect call, don't do it.

One Last Tip
Practice.
Listen to yourself.
Keep at it.
It does get easier.

How Am I Doing So Far?

Go ahead and skip this page if you want to. But it's easy, so why don't you take a shot at it.

Five adjectives I would use to describe myself:

_____ _____ _____

_____ _____

The skills I most want to use on the job are:

_____

_____

_____

When I think about interviewing I feel _____
because _____ .

List three things to keep close to your telephone.

1. _____ 2. _____ 3. _____

The biggest obstacle in my job search is _____ .

Two things I can do to minimize it are _____
and _____ .

Contacts that are already a part of my network are _____
_____ and _____ .

Contacts I need to make are _____ and

_____ .

Job sources I plan to use immediately:

_____ _____ _____

Don't stop now. Keep reading . . .

PROMOTING YOUR PRODUCT WITH A RESUME

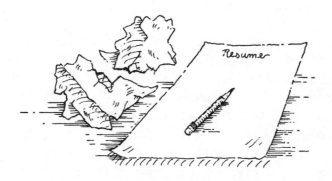

This Chapter Is For Everyone.
That Includes You.

Cooks, cashiers, clerks, and caretakers need resumes.

Doctors, dentists, drummers, and ditch-diggers need them.

Tellers, technicians, teachers, traffic controllers, and truckdrivers need them.

Housewives, househusbands, horse trainers, and horticulturists need them, too.

And so do you. You need to introduce yourself to someone who can hire you. That's one of the things a resume can help you to do.

You can use it as an Oversized Calling Card. It tells the employer:

- who you are
- what you've done
- what you can do

> **Andy Applicant**
> Address
> Skills
> Qualifications
> Interests

A resume is more than an introduction. You can use it as a crib sheet when you're filling out application forms. It's also a handy checklist when you're talking to an employer on the telephone.

Your resume is a valuable marketing tool, and don't let your status or your job objective keep you from using it.

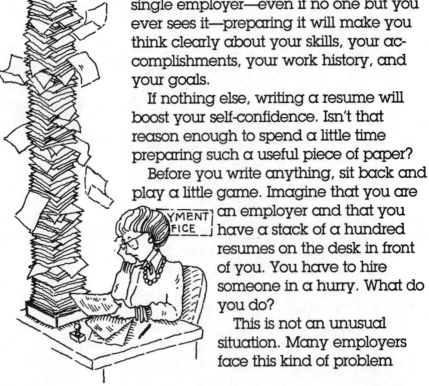

Even if you never show your resume to a single employer—even if no one but you ever sees it—preparing it will make you think clearly about your skills, your accomplishments, your work history, and your goals.

If nothing else, writing a resume will boost your self-confidence. Isn't that reason enough to spend a little time preparing such a useful piece of paper?

Before you write anything, sit back and play a little game. Imagine that you are an employer and that you have a stack of a hundred resumes on the desk in front of you. You have to hire someone in a hurry. What do you do?

This is not an unusual situation. Many employers face this kind of problem routinely. To help them skim the resumes and make some decisions, they want to be able to get the information they need with as little effort as possible.

Resumes are **not:**

I mystery stories
I autobiographies
I obituaries
I personal essays
I philosophical statements

●◆ Employers want **resumes that are easy to read.**

●◆ Employers want **truthful resumes.**

●◆ Employers want **accurate resumes.**

●◆ Employers want **relevant resumes.**

●◆ Employers want **current resumes.**

●◆ Employers want **error-free resumes.**

●◆ Employers want **concise resumes.**

and . . .

●◆ Employers want **resumes that look good.**

Painless Resume Preparation

Writing a resume is not especially difficult; it's much easier than filling out tax forms or credit applications, and you don't have to be a great writer to put together a good one.

Get a pencil and a piece of paper. Put your name and address at the top. You've already written 10 to 20 percent of your resume.

What follows next depends on your past. Some of you might need as few as three or four section headings; others might need seven or eight. Choose those you need to tell an employer about you.

Build on your strengths. The first heading listed on your resume should be the item you most want an employer to notice. If you are considering several very different kinds of jobs, you can prepare more than one version of your resume to emphasize the experiences and skills appropriate to each kind of job. See pages 83–88 for a variety of sample resumes.

Any of the following words or phrases might help tell your story.

SECTION HEADINGS

Competencies

Areas of Expertise

Areas of Knowledge

Objective

Job Objective

Employment Objective

Position Desired

Current Employment

Employment

Employment Record

Employment History

Work History

Experience

Experience Summary

Additional Experience

Related Experience

Other Work

Part-Time Work

Military Service

Skills	Community Services
Special Skills	Community Involvement
Computer Skills	Community and Other
Writing Skills	Activities
Speaking Skills	
Leadership Skills	Interests
Organizational Skills	Special Talents
Administrative Skills	Personal Interests
Technical Skills	Leisure Activities
Personal Attributes	Education
Activities	Educational Background
Achievements	Educational Preparation
Accomplishments	Training
Honors and Awards	Certificates
Distinctions	Licenses
	Special Training
Volunteer Activities	Continuing Education
Related Activities	Recent Courses
Civic Activities	Courses of Interest

Personal data—age, height, weight, spouse's occupation, marital status, number of children, and religious affiliation—have no place on a resume. You want to be judged on your skills, competencies, and experiences, not on irrelevant personal information.

THE 30-SECOND TEST

Keep in mind that the employer probably won't read every word. Most will spend about 30 seconds with each resume. That's right—30 seconds. That's a discouraging (even disgusting) thought given the time you spend in writing your resume, but it's no exaggeration. So— since you have only 30 seconds to catch the employer's attention—make your resume worth the reading.

Keep It Simple

The best resumes are as short as they can be; they don't have extra words, complex sentences, or long paragraphs of text. Sentence fragments are perfectly acceptable—and even desirable—because they eliminate the need for beginning each line with "I was . . ." "I did . . ." "I have . . ."

Make It Come Alive

The words you choose can make your resume read easily and quickly, or they can make it lumber along. Don't be passive. Express your accomplishments and achievements in dynamic, meaningful words. "Action words" will help to give your resume life and energy.

ACTION WORDS

Accomplished	Evaluated	Participated
Acquired	Expanded	Performed
Administered	Headed	Planned
Analyzed	Implemented	Prepared
Arranged	Improved	Presented
Assessed	Increased	Presided
Assisted	Initiated	Promoted
Chosen	Instituted	Produced
Communicated	Introduced	Represented
Completed	Invented	Revised
Conducted	Investigated	Scheduled
Controlled	Led	Selected
Coordinated	Maintained	Sold
Created	Managed	Solved
Designed	Mastered	Sponsored
Developed	Moderated	Strengthened
Directed	Motivated	Supervised
Earned	Negotiated	Streamlined
Elected	Organized	Trained
Established	Operated	Volunteered

Blow Your Own Horn

A good resume is not shy or modest about stating accomplishments, skills, and past experiences. If you don't tell the reader what you've done, who will? But don't get carried away. Exaggerations, deceptions, or even the slightest misrepresentation can, if discovered, eliminate you from consideration. If you've already been hired, these discrepancies could be cause for dismissal.

Stick to the Point

Don't be excessively detailed, either. You might have had a dozen or more different jobs in the last 20 or 30 years. A resume is not the place to list each and every one of them with corresponding dates. Be selective.

> *During a 15-year span, Kevin had 17 different jobs. Some of them he felt good about; some he'd just as soon forget. He was worried about listing all these jobs on his resume. Would he be lying if he listed some but not others?*

The solution to Kevin's problem is fairly simple. Without misrepresenting himself, he summarized his experiences this way:

> **From 1970 to 1985, full-time and part-time jobs included waiter, house-painter, city bus driver, motel clerk, and security officer.**

Kevin didn't clutter his resume or bore the reader with meaningless places and dates. He didn't waste valuable space on odd jobs that had no relevance to his current goals. He didn't try to hide anything, but he did account for his time, and he gave the employer sufficient information to provide a basis for further inquiry.

Write It Right

You want your resume to stand out from the others. You want it to be noticed. You don't want it to be noticed for the wrong reasons: spelling errors, incorrect grammar, or improper vocabulary. Check, recheck, and then have someone else check it, too.

Keep It Clean

Your resume shouldn't look like a used place mat. Coffee stains, ketchup smears, grease spots, or unidentifiable smudges will launch it toward its final resting place—the garbage can. Spindled, mutilated, or otherwise abused pieces of paper are easy for employers to discard.

As obvious as this may seem, you would be amazed at the number of obviously used resumes employers receive. Recycling is not in your best interest in this case. Simply put,

If Your Resume Doesn't Look Good, Neither Do You!!

Production Made Easy

Most job seekers will need multiple copies of a resume. You have better things to do with your time than to type each one individually; you can choose from several different production methods. An easy way is to have your typed copy photographically reproduced. Print shops can give you better quality reproduction than the copy machine at the drugstore or bank, and the cost should be about the same or even less.

Computer-generated resumes are certainly acceptable, and if you have a personal computer or have access to one, by all means use it. Updating is easy, and you can adjust the layout and reorganize categories as needed.

Professional typesetting is always an option—and always the most expensive. It's easy, you don't have to know how to type, and the finished product is usually of high quality. Because of the typesetting process, updates and alterations are costly and can take time. Typesetting does offer greater flexibility and wider choices for size and style of print than most other methods. Look at the samples of point sizes and type styles.

Point Sizes

6
8
10
11
12
14
18

24
30
36
48

60
72

Type Styles

Avant Garde Book
Avant Garde Bold

Bookman Medium
Bookman Bold
Bookman Italic

Century Textbook
Century Textbook Bold
Century Textbook Italic

Helvetica Regular
Helvetica Bold
Helvetica Italic

Helvetica Condensed
Helvetica Bold Condensed

Lubalin Graph Book
Lubalin Graph Demi
Lubalin Graph Italic
Lubalin Graph Demi Italic

Palatino Regular
Palatino Bold
Palatino Italic

Times Roman Book
Times Roman Bold
Times Roman Italic

Zapf Chancery

Quality Is the Best Gimmick

However your resume is produced, don't settle for anything less than a quality product: good, dark print on attractive bond paper of standard size. White paper is always safe; soft, neutral colors are fine, too. Bright, flashy colors, whimsical graphics, odd sizes, and unusual folding simply don't work. The best gimmick to catch an employer's attention is an attractive, well-organized resume with no mistakes.

DON'T LEAVE HOME WITHOUT IT

Take your resume with you. You never know whom you are going to see or what opportunities may come your way. Always send a resume with a cover letter when you inquire about a position or apply for a job. Submit a resume along with a completed application form. Take extra copies along to interviews. Give a copy to each person in your job-search network. A person who has agreed to serve as a reference will find a copy of your resume helpful. A resume is a great marketing tool, so spread it around.

Pick and Choose

Read through the following sample resumes. Notice the layout, the section headings, the action words, and the organization of each resume. Notice, too, how the different methods of organization emphasize work history, qualifications, skills, or preparation.

Use the samples as guides rather than as models to be followed precisely. You might adapt one of these formats, or you might combine the features of two or more of them to create a resume that will represent you.

✓ Keep your resume simple.

✓ Emphasize your strengths.

✓ Make your resume work for you.

Vera E. Goode

R.R. 2, Box 27
New Royal, Iowa 50268
(712-398-5020)

PERSONAL ATTRIBUTES

Responsible   Energetic
Trustworthy   Flexible
Organized   Courteous

ACCOMPLISHMENTS

Managed finances of multifaceted agricultural
business

Elected to church governing board

Supervised and judged youth projects for state
fair competition

Selected as political representative for county
convention

COMMUNITY INVOLVEMENT

Planning member, New Royal's centennial
celebration

Host family, AFS student from New Zealand,
2 years

Volunteer, community fire fighters' association

Co-leader, Cub Scout troop

Participant, county soil conservation project

EDUCATIONAL BACKGROUND

Marshalltown High School, Marshalltown, Iowa

Garfield County Extension Services, Frederick,
Iowa, Extension Courses and Workshops

REFERENCES AVAILABLE ON REQUEST

BEA REDDY

1809 Davenport Road
San Jose, California 95193
(408) 277-0105

SKILLS: Repair/restore antique furniture
                   Woodworking
                   Cabinetmaking
                   Stripping and refinishing

EXPERIENCE: Free-lance restoring and refinishing, 1984-

                   Specializing in fine wood items (mantel clocks,
                   jewelry boxes, picture frames).

                   Handyman's Hardware, St. Louis, Missouri, 1976-80

                   Sales clerk in paint and home repair departments.
                   Assisted and advised customers; responsible for
                   inventory, pricing, and helping manager with
                   department layout and merchandise display.

                   Charlie's Cabinets & Millwork, Rolla, Missouri,
                   1968-74

                   Began as apprentice in family business (part-time
                   until 1970). Advanced to full responsibility for
                   projects, including preparation of estimates and
                   contracts. Repaired and restored valuable
                   antique furniture; built and installed kitchen
                   and bathroom cabinets, with special emphasis on
                   renovating 19th-century houses.

HOBBIES: Antique furniture and glassware
                   Rosemaling
                   Needlework

EDUCATION: Rolla High School, Rolla, Missouri, 1967-70
                   (diploma)

REFERENCES: Available upon request.

Hiram E. Soon

4829 Park Avenue
Baton Rouge, Louisiana 70802
(504) 203-7096

Competencies

- Developing and evaluating ideas
- Motivating and persuading others
- Using technology to streamline

- Managing time, people and projects
- Communicating on paper and in person
- Prioritizing large volumes of work

Recent Courses of Interest

Design and Management of Organizations
Computer Applications - IBM, Apple
Training and Development
Investment Management
Communications in Human Resource Management

Leadership & Accomplishments

- Selected to participate in National Leadership Institute for Young Professionals
- Co-authored and received grant for computer-assisted data collection
- Developed workshops & conferences with participants ranging from graduate students to local business leaders
- Supervised six merit employees and ten work-study students
- Received Governor's Volunteer Award, 1988
- Represented neighborhood on City Advisory Council
- Advised executive council and elected members of student government
- Trained state tennis competitors
- Traveled and studied in Europe and Middle East

Professional Experience

Assistant Registrar, Louisiana State University, Baton Rouge, 1989-present

History/Science Teacher and Head Tennis Coach, Lake Forest, Illinois, 1983-1987

Academic Training

The University of Iowa, Iowa City, Iowa, Master of Arts Degree, 1989

Mankato State University, Mankato, Minnesota, Bachelor of Arts Degree, 1983

Awards & Activities

Graduated Cum Laude
Senior Scholarship, Mankato State University
Student body president, Mankato State University
Tennis letterman and captain, Mankato State University
Graduate Student Senate representative
Strommen Graduate Fellowship Award, The University of Iowa
Committee member, Central Parks and Recreation Board
President, Mississippi Wildlife Preservation Committee

References provided upon request

ANNIE APPLICANT

R.R. 2, BOX 21
IDAHO FALLS, IDAHO 83401
208-387-1025

**APPOINTMENTS
& ACTIVITIES**

School Board Member (1986-present), Valley
 School District, Idaho Falls, Idaho.
 Elected Board president in 1988. Responsibilities include overseeing financial
 responsibility, evaluating administrative
 performance, projecting future needs, and
 maintaining district goals of educational
 excellence.

Board of Directors, Norseman Community Theatre
 (1983-1987), Idaho Falls, Idaho. Responsibilities included fund raising, promoting
 area actors and performances, maintaining
 community link to area college representa-
 tives, and organizing and co-directing the
 children's theatre.

County Supervisor, Shawnee County (1977-1981),
 Topeka, Kansas. Responsibilities included
 improving county services (ranging from road
 maintenance to instituting new policies and
 procedures for county health-care facility),
 hiring and evaluating personnel, strengthen-
 ing bonds with local city councils, and
 planning future projects.

COMPETENCIES

Public Relations	Financial Management
Organizational Skills	Program Development

DEGREE

Kansas State University, Manhattan, Kansas
Bachelor of Arts degree, 1972
Major: Communications

CIVIC INTERESTS

Member, Idaho Falls Hospital Planning Committee
Director, Idaho Falls Church Choir
Participant, Eastern Idaho United Nations
 Organization
Past President, Tri-State Women's Consulting
 Group
Volunteer, Valley Hospital

REFERENCES

B. J. Blakeley, County Attorney (398-4769)
Charlotte Smith, Former School Board President
 (387-5001)
Dr. Glen Sorensen, Dean, Eastern Idaho
 Community College (387-9203)
John Haman, Administrator, Valley Hospital
 (387-1079)

KEN DUITT

461 West Fifth Street
Beatrice, Nebraska 68310
(402) 561-2834

CURRENT EMPLOYMENT

Self-employed independent moving service operator, 1987-
Local and long-distance transfers.

WORK HISTORY

Truck Driver, Rowley Interstate Trucking Company, Beatrice,
Nebraska, 1980-87.
Specialized in transporting perishable goods. Responsible
for maintenance of assigned equipment, scheduling pickups
and deliveries. Maintained accurate D.O.T. records, log
books, and handled permits and invoices.

Truck Driver, Husker Moving Company, Lincoln, Nebraska, 1974-80.
Responsible for packing and moving furniture and household
goods.

Taxi Driver, Red & White Taxi Company, Lincoln, Nebraska, 1972-74.
Part-time driver, evenings and weekends.

MILITARY EXPERIENCE

U.S. Air Force, 1968-72. Assigned to motor pool, Fort Leonard
Wood, Missouri. Honorable discharge. E-4 rating.

EDUCATION AND TRAINING

Diesel Truck Driver Training School, Norfolk, Nebraska, July 1974.

Southeast Community College, Lincoln, Nebraska, 1972-73.
Completed one year of general studies program.

Beatrice Senior High School, Beatrice, Nebraska, high school
diploma, 1968.

REFERENCES

Available upon request.

Will B. Abel

21 Park Avenue North
Annapolis, Maryland 21406
(301) 263-9351

CURRENT EMPLOYMENT

Insurance Sales, Senior Representative, Eastern States
Mutual, Annapolis, Maryland, 1987 - present

EMPLOYMENT OVERVIEW

INSURANCE SALES	10 YEARS
COMPUTER INSTRUCTOR & STORE MANAGER	7 YEARS
TELEPHONE SALES	4 YEARS

ACCOMPLISHMENTS

Member, Board of Directors, Annapolis Public Library
Awarded Silver Beaver Medal, Boy Scouts of America
Elected President of local service club
Organized community-wide service drive for deserving
  children
Named outstanding young business leader by Annapolis
  business community

EDUCATION

Bunker Hill Community College, Boston, Massachusetts

    A.A. Degree 1968
        Honors: Dean's List
        Who's Who in American Junior Colleges
        Letterman--Football and Baseball

    Sales Seminars and Workshops 1985 - present

        Sales and Communication, Loyola College
        Management Series, University of Maryland
          at Baltimore
        Leadership Strategies, Springfield Technical
        Center

REFERENCES

John Wilken, Eastern Regional Insurance Director,
  Frederick, Maryland (301) 694-5989

T.J. Hildebrand, Associate Professor, University of
  Maryland at Baltimore (301) 528-4121

Resume of
Ima Ruffdraft

Turn back to the Section Headings on pages 74–75. Pick 5 words or phrases to get you started. Now, write what you can under each heading. This is your first rough draft—don't worry about how it looks. After you get the basics on paper you can add, subtract, rearrange, and revise on your way to a finished product.

✍ PROMOTING YOUR PRODUCT BY LETTER

*L*etters are not yet extinct, though they may be an endangered species. We call our parents, we call our children, we call out for pizza, and—often—we call employers to apply for jobs. Why take the time to write when the telephone is so handy?

Telephone calls and personal visits are both effective ways to find jobs. For some types of jobs, the best way to apply is just to show up ready to talk about your skills—maybe even ready to go to work. For other jobs you can stop by, leave a copy of your resume, and fill out an application form. Using these two methods alone will put you in the running for quite a few jobs, especially those in your immediate vicinity. What about the others?

If you're looking for jobs in other communities, writing letters is the most economical and effective way to apply. Even for local jobs, many employers prefer to receive letters even though it takes time to read them, file them, or respond to them.

> ***Natassia Norman needs to hire a clerk and a secretary/ receptionist for her expanding business. She can't afford to interrupt her activities to talk to walk-ins. Letters of application can be screened at her convenience—at the office or even at home. Also, Natassia can use the letters to determine whether applicants have a good knowledge of grammar, spelling, and sentence structure. She can narrow the field to a select few and invite them to interview for the jobs.***

Simply put, a letter is a powerful marketing technique. Your letter represents you, introduces you, and can open the door for an interview—if it makes a positive first impression.

An effective letter tells who you are and what you can do and makes the employer want to meet you. A poor letter tells too much or too little and quickly finds its way into the employer's rejection stack.

But I Haven't Written a Letter in Years

Don't think you can't write a good letter. If you haven't written a business letter for years, you might be reluctant to try. People make lots of excuses.

✘ I don't have time.

✘ I can't type (or I don't have a typewriter).

✘ I'd rather use the telephone.

✘ I don't know what to say.

✘ I'd rather apply in person.

✘ Writing to a stranger is too difficult, and
   I don't know who to send it to anyway.

Just the thought of writing letters creates anxiety for many job seekers. If you're one of them, you're probably concerned about how to start and what to say. Employers aren't interested in fancy phrases or creative approaches. They want only the basics: why you're writing and what you have to offer. And remember that you'll usually include your resume with any letter about a specific job.

If you can't type your letters, find a good friend to type them for you, or hire someone. It doesn't cost much, and it's one of the best investments you can make. Even the neatest handwritten letter should be only a last resort.

The following samples illustrate the three types of letters you'll need in a job search:

➤ **letter of inquiry**
   to ask if positions are available or anticipated

➤ **letter of application**
   in response to an advertisement

➤ **letter following an interview**

Job seekers who can't or won't use these marketing tools effectively close the door to many opportunities.

LETTER OF INQUIRY

421 8th Street
Yuma, Arizona 85292
February 15, 1991

Personnel Department
West Essex General Hospital
P.O. Box 1940
Livingston, New Jersey 07039

I am writing to inquire if you anticipate any openings in your respiratory therapy department. In
April I will be moving to New Jersey, and I am
interested in employment in your area.

As you will note from the enclosed resume, I have
been working as a respiratory therapist at the Yuma
Medical Center for five years. Currently I am working with cardiac patients, but I have had the opportunity to deal with a wide range of respiratory
disorders. I enjoy working with patients of all
ages, and I have been successful in teaching patients and family members to learn new techniques to
aid in improving their conditions.

In addition to my initial training in San Diego, I
have accumulated twelve Continuing Education Units
and have attended a variety of seminars and workshops to update my specialty. I feel confident that
I could contribute to your therapy department at
West Essex General Hospital.

If you anticipate any openings in respiratory therapy, please inform me of application procedures. I
will be visiting in the area during the week of
March 5 and would welcome the opportunity to interview at that time.

Yvonne Vallejo

Enc.

> **Note:**
> Simplified style of business letter
> (no salutation, no complimentary closing)
> Full block style; margins flush to the left
> Requests application materials or procedures
> Resume enclosed

LETTER OF APPLICATION

```
                          141 N. Wilder
                          St. Paul, Minnesota 55107
                          September 12, 1991
```

Marguerite Grant
Administrative Associate
Marsha Kenneth Library
White Bear Lake Community College
White Bear Lake, Minnesota 55110

Dear Ms. Grant:

Please consider me an applicant for the Library
Assistant position advertised in the September 11th
edition of the *St. Paul Pioneer Press.* I am available for immediate employment, and I feel that my
qualifications match your needs.

Your ad states that typing skills are required. I am
familiar with most standard typewriters, including
electronic memory typewriters, and I have some
experience with word processing on personal computers. My typing speed is 70 words per minute with a
high degree of accuracy. My schedule is flexible and
I could work evenings and weekends as required.

My resume briefly outlines my recent activities and
interests. I would be happy to come in for an interview at your convenience. I look forward to hearing
from you.

Sincerely yours,

Mark Wong

Enc.

> **Note:**
> Modified block style; return address and
> closing to the right
> Job opening identified
> Qualifications presented
> Interest in interview expressed
> Resume enclosed

INTERVIEW FOLLOW-UP

23 Pleasant Street
Monroe, Louisiana 71201
December 7, 1991

Adam Lougaris
Employment Supervisor
United Discounts, Inc.
7800 Industrial Parkway
Baton Rouge, Louisiana 70829

Dear Mr. Lougaris:

I appreciated the opportunity to interview for
the position in your accounting department on December 5. Your plans for expansion of your computer
installation, as explained by you and Marian Berg,
are innovative, and I feel I could make an immediate
contribution to their success. I am very interested
in the job, and I want to be considered a serious
candidate for the position.

Thank you for the time and consideration. Meeting you and your staff, and touring your facilities,
was a real pleasure. I look forward to hearing from
you soon.

Sincerely,

Kim Vercande

Note:
Modified block style with indented
paragraphs
Sent shortly after the interview
Reinforces items discussed at interview
Expresses continued interest in the job

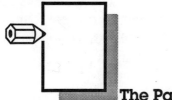

The Paper Image

Don't agonize over a catchy opening or an attention-grabbing first sentence. Get it out of the way quickly. There's nothing wrong with just stating the facts.

> "I would like to apply for the position of administrative assistant advertised in the March 28th issue of the *Minneapolis Tribune*."

> "Please consider me as an applicant for the cashier's position listed with the Community Job Line."

> "Because of my fifteen years in food service, I feel qualified for the job of Catering Supervisor recently posted in your personnel department."

Each of these openings tells the reader the purpose of the letter, the position being applied for, and how the writer learned about the vacancy. Employers are too busy to play guessing games. Don't wait until the end of your letter to tell them why you're writing.

The middle part of your letter should state that your resume is enclosed, but don't stop there. Increase your chances of being noticed by briefly highlighting qualifications or experiences that directly relate to the available job.

The last paragraph is easy. Let the employer know you want the job and that you are available for an interview.

✓ Sign it.
✓ Seal it.
✓ Send it.

You've just applied for a job.

And you've just increased your chances of being hired. Some people won't take the time to write a letter. Others are convinced it's too difficult. And still others will write letters that are less effective than yours.

Avoiding the Circular File

Ask any employer about the impact of cover letters. You'll get responses ranging from amused chuckles to outraged howls. And you'll hear about letters they have received and immediately dismissed: form letters; hand-written notes; letters with spelling errors, poor grammar, incorrect names and addresses; and letters that have been improperly folded, spindled, or otherwise mutilated.

Your letter will make a good first impression because it's clear, concise, and correct. It focuses on the job and your qualifications. It's typed on good quality, standard-sized 8 1/2-by-11-inch paper, it follows a recognized business format, and it can be read (or at least scanned) in a minute or two. No employer is going to take seriously a communication on

- *a post card*
- *flowered or scented stationery*
- *a sheet of memo-pad paper with cute sayings or cartoon characters*
- *loud, glaring colored paper*

These gimmicks will get attention, but not the right kind. The reader might chuckle about them over coffee with a colleague, but they'll end up with the rest of the junk mail.

Looking good on paper can literally mean the difference between being considered for a job or being pushed aside.

The Last Step

Folding your letter (and resume) properly can make a difference in how it looks to the employer. Don't staple it together or use any type of fastener; it's harder to file, rips or snags easily, and wrecks automatic letter openers.

Most business letters use a #10 envelope, especially if more than one page is enclosed. When you send your resume, your letter should cover your resume and the two should be folded together, like this:

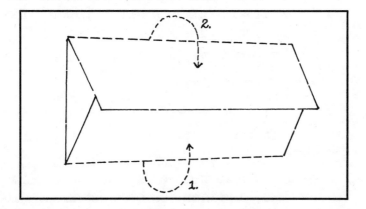

Although a larger envelope is preferable, it is permissible to use a #6 envelope for a single sheet of paper. For a small envelope, fold your letter like this:

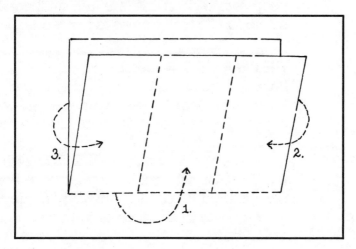

To Whom It May Concern

Salutations are important because they contribute to a favorable first impression. Whenever possible, address your letter to a specific person. If the ad says to contact John Smith, you write a "Dear Mr. Smith" letter. But what do you do if it's not so clear cut?

You'd like to apply for a job you've just read about in the newspaper. The ad instructs you to contact "B. J. Jones." Which of the following is the best salutation?

Dear Mr. Jones

Dear Ms. Jones

Dear Sir or Madam

Dear B. J. Jones

There's only one good answer—the last one. B. J. could stand for Billy Joe or Barbara Jean, and many Barbara Jeans don't like to be addressed as Dear Sir.

When in doubt, use the full name. Don't assume that only men are in charge of hiring people, and don't assume that an incorrect salutation doesn't matter to the reader.

THE DEAR SIR SYNDROME

It used to be standard practice to begin a letter with "Dear Sir," even if the name was known. Times have changed. Use the name if you know it, and if you don't have a name, don't assume the reader is a man. If the "Dear Sir" who receives your letter happens to be a "Dear Ms.," she may not read your letter with as much enthusiasm as it deserves.

Never risk losing the reader's attention by using an outdated or inappropriate salutation. "Dear Sir" is probably the most common error, but some other salutations should be avoided, too.

Dead-end Dears

Dear Sir	Dear Friends
Dear Sir/Madam	Dear Personnel
Gentlemen	Dear Director
Dear Ma'am	Hello!
Dear Gentlepeople	Good Morning!
Dear People	To Whom It May
Dear Reader	Concern

A SIMPLE SOLUTION

What if there is no name at all? More and more ads are nameless. You might be instructed to contact a company, a personnel office, even a box number. If you don't know the name of the person you're writing to, don't revert to one of the "Dead-end Dears." There is a much better and much simpler approach. It's called the *simplified style of business letter*, and it omits both the salutation and any complimentary closing (such as "Sincerely yours"). You'll find an example on page 94.

The simplified style of business letter is useful in many situations, but it can be especially helpful during a job search. It eliminates uncertainty, saves time, and is sure to look good. Use it whenever you don't have the full name of the contact person.

APPLICATION FORMS

You've filled out application forms before, perhaps more of them than you'd like to remember. You know by now that some are relatively simple; others are spread out over several pages and seem to ask endless questions. Some are slick, attractive packages; others look as if they were hastily thrown together and cheaply reproduced. But many of them look alike and sound alike, and because they ask the same routine questions, filling them out can be pretty boring.

Whether the application form looks important or not, it is worth taking seriously. Don't let the appearance mislead you, and don't take shortcuts. It is not sufficient to write "See attached resume" across the form and hand it back. Employers don't like paperwork any more than you do, but they expect applicants to cooperate. It is always a good idea to submit your resume along with your completed application form, but take the time to provide the information requested on the form. It will pay off.

The application form is one of the most common devices for screening applicants. Employers use the forms to obtain comparable information from each applicant. The uniform pattern of responses allows the employer to locate essential information quickly, without having to search through a resume or make verbal inquiries. It's an efficient way for employers to compare skills and qualifications.

Some applicants make the employer's task even easier by rushing through the form, scrawling their responses, skipping some items, and giving sketchy answers to others. The employer is likely to give a poorly prepared application form equally casual treatment and move on to one that is legible, complete, and informative. Why take chances when it's just as easy to do a good job?

Read It First

Many people have problems with application forms because they jump right in and start filling out the form only to discover they haven't followed directions. Take your time. Read through the entire form before you begin writing. The few minutes it takes can save you a lot of time.

Problem Questions

Most parts of an application form are straightforward and easy to answer, but some items may pose problems. Although affirmative action and equal employment opportunity guidelines for pre-employment inquiries have been around for a long time, some application forms don't reflect them. You may still find some applications that ask about your age, religion, race, and national origin.

Questions that may not be illegal but are clearly inappropriate are ones about marital status, number of dependents, height, weight, color of eyes and hair, parent's address, occupation of parents or spouse, whether you

own or rent, whether you live alone, and personal financial statements including assets and debts.

For most jobs, these items are not relevant. In some
instances, however, some of this information could be job
related. For example, a model could be expected to
answer questions about height, weight, and coloring. But
a computer technician's qualifications are not determined by the inch, the pound, or the color of hair.

Answering Problem Questions

If you encounter questions that seem to have no relevance to the job for which you are applying, you do
have options. Obviously, you can choose to answer the
questions. If you prefer not to give the information, don't
just leave the item blank. Put in a dash (—), which will
indicate that you have read the question, or write in
"N/A," which means "Not Applicable" (or, in this case,
"Not Appropriate").

Another option is to put an asterisk (*) in the space and,
at the end of the form, put the following statement: "Answers will be provided upon employment." Keep in mind
that once you are hired, the employer will need certain
information for insurance policies and emergency
contacts.

Many application forms will raise other questions that
present problems for some job seekers. For example,
there might be questions about reasons for leaving previous jobs, physical or mental disabilities, or criminal records. If any of these situations applies to you, keep three
things in mind:

1. Tell the Truth
Employers do carry out background checks. Misrepresenting your past can eliminate you from consideration or can be grounds for immediate dismissal.

2. Keep Your Answers Brief and Positive
Tell employers what they need to know. Elaborate self-justifications or sob stories won't help.

3. Use Words Employers Can Understand
Use layman's language rather than technical terms or medical jargon. Keep your explanations simple. Don't expect employers to get out their dictionaries.

ASK FOR AN INTERVIEW

You have a better chance of convincing an employer to hire you if you can tell your story in person. Attach a note to the application form indicating that you would like to discuss your work record, your disability, your criminal record, or any other problem area.

Questions about Money

It's not uncommon for employment applications to contain questions about previous earnings, salary history, or salary expectations. If you are asked to state your earnings on previous jobs, tell the truth. But it is permissible to round off figures and to include the value of benefits you received.

In response to questions about your expected earnings, you should not feel obligated to state a dollar figure. "Negotiable" is the best and most comprehensive term to use. It leaves all the doors open, and you are not put in the position of overpricing or undervaluing your skills.

\$\$ If you know that wages for the job are set by a contract between the employer and the employees' union or bargaining unit, you may simply indicate "per schedule."

\$\$ If "negotiable" and "per schedule" won't work and you must give a dollar figure, use a range rather than an exact amount.

Beyond Filling in the Blanks

Questions that simply require you to fill in the blanks are the easiest, but sometimes you will be asked to write a paragraph or even more. You may be asked to state why you want to work for this company; other questions may deal with your specific skills; or there may be a very broad question, such as "Write a paragraph about yourself."

Certainly, what you say is important. But the way you express yourself can have equal or even greater impact. Employers use this type of question to take a careful look at your spelling, grammar, and ability to write complete sentences and logical paragraphs.

Don't be afraid of these short "essay" questions. There is no "right answer"; all they're asking for is an example of your writing. If you have the chance, work out your response on a piece of scratch paper, and then transfer it neatly to the application form. Never skip over these questions. They can make a big difference.

References and Recommendations

Many application forms ask you to provide names of current or previous employers, or other people who have knowledge of your abilities or character. Be ready to supply names, addresses, and phone numbers of people who can provide recommendations on your behalf. Before you list individuals' names, tell them you're looking for a job and get their OK. If they're aware of your intentions, they'll be better able to support your application. This is especially true if you list your current employer as a reference. Surprises can work against you; don't take the chance of letting your current employer learn from someone else that you are looking for a job.

Many employers will only verify employment status and dates of employment. Some will provide written letters of recommendation that you can share with hiring officials. If your employer or supervisor gives you a written recommendation, make photocopies of it to be submitted with application materials or presented at an interview.

Typical Application Forms

The following samples are typical of the kinds of application forms employers are using today.

SEARS, ROEBUCK AND CO.
APPLICATION FOR EMPLOYMENT

SEARS IS AN EQUAL OPPORTUNITY EMPLOYER and fully subscribes to the principles of Equal Employment Opportunity. Sears has adopted an Affirmative Action Program to ensure that all applicants and employees are considered for hire, promotion and job status, without regard to race, color, religion, sex, age, national origin, handicap or status as a disabled veteran or veteran of the Vietnam Era.

NOTE: This application will be considered active for 90 days. If you have not been employed within this period and are still interested in employment at Sears, please contact the office where you applied and request that your application be reactivated.

PLEASE PRINT
Personal Data

Print Name in full _____ Social Security Number _____
    (Last)   (First)   (Middle)

Home address _____ Telephone _____
    (Street) (City) (State) (Zip Code)

Temporary address _____ Telephone _____
    (Street) (City) (State) (Zip Code)

If hired, can you furnish proof of age? ☐ YES ☐ NO

(Answer only if position for which you are applying requires driving.)
    Licensed to drive car? ☐ YES ☐ NO
    Is license valid in this State? ☐ YES ☐ NO

If hired, can you furnish proof you are legally entitled to work in U.S.
    ☐ YES ☐ NO

Have you ever been employed by Sears? ☐ YES ☐ NO
If so, when and where last employed? _____
Position _____
Are any of your relatives employed by Sears? ☐ NO ☐ YES
If so, in which unit(s) are they employed? _____

Type of position desired? _____
Date available for work _____
State salary you will consider _____
Are you willing to relocate? _____
What initial location would you prefer? _____
Have you been convicted of a felony involving life or property during the past seven
years?   ☐ NO   ☐ YES
If yes, explain _____

Physical Data

A PHYSICAL OR MENTAL DISABILITY WILL NOT CAUSE REJECTION IF IN SEARS
MEDICAL OPINION YOU ARE ABLE TO SATISFACTORILY PERFORM IN THE POSI-
TION FOR WHICH YOU ARE BEING CONSIDERED.

Do you have any physical condition which may limit your ability to perform the job
applied for? If so, please give details. _____
Do you have any Service related disability?   ☐ NO   ☐ YES

**To protect the interests of all concerned, applicants for certain job assignments
must pass a physical examination before they are hired. Alternative placement of an
applicant who does not meet the physical standards of the job for which he/she was
originally considered is permitted.**

Education

	No. of Years	Name of School	City and State	Course or College Major	Average Grades	Did you graduate?	Type of Degree
Senior High School							
College							
Graduate Studies							
Other— Give Type							

Military Service

Branch of Service   Service-related Skills and Experience Applicable to Civilian Employment
_____   _____

Activities

Professional Organizations _____
What are your hobbies or special interests? _____

Experience

Please give a detailed account of your previous experience and training. Specify the type
of work done and the type of work you would prefer to do. If more space is needed, continue
on a supplementary page. _____
_____
_____

110

RECORD OF EMPLOYMENT AND REFERENCES

LIST BELOW YOUR FOUR MOST RECENT EMPLOYERS, BEGINNING WITH THE CURRENT OR MOST RECENT ONE. IF YOU HAVE HAD LESS THAN FOUR EMPLOYERS, USE THE REMAINING SPACES FOR PERSONAL REFERENCES. IF YOU WERE EMPLOYED UNDER A MAIDEN NAME OR OTHER NAME, PLEASE ENTER THAT NAME IN THE RIGHT-HAND MARGIN. IF APPLICABLE, ENTER SERVICE IN THE ARMED FORCES ON THE REVERSE SIDE.

☐ It is not satisfactory to contact my present employer.
☐ It is satisfactory to contact my present employer.

NOTE: State reason for and length of inactivity between present application date and last employer.					Nature of Employer's Business	Name of your Supervisor
Name						
Address			Tel. No.			
City		State	Zip Code			
What kind of work did you do?	Starting Date	Starting Pay	Date of Leaving	Pay at Leaving	Why did you leave? Give details	
	Month	$ ☐ Mo	Month	$ ☐ Mo		
	Year	☐ Wk. ☐ Hr.	Year	☐ Wk. ☐ Hr.		

I certify that the information contained in this application is correct to the best of my knowledge and understand that any misstatement or omission of information is grounds for dismissal in accordance with Sears, Roebuck and Co. policy. I authorize the references listed above to give you any and all information concerning my previous employment and any pertinent information they may have, personal or otherwise, and release all parties from all liability for any damage that may result from furnishing same to you. In consideration of my employment, I agree to conform to the rules and regulations of Sears, Roebuck and Co. and my employment and compensation can be terminated with our without cause and with or without notice, at any time, at the option of either the Company or myself. I understand that no unit manager or representative of Sears, Roebuck and Co. other than the President or Vice-President of the Company, has any authority to enter into any agreement for employment for any specified period of time, or to make any agreement contrary to the foregoing. In some states, the law requires that Sears have my written permission before obtaining consumer reports on me, and I hereby authorize Sears to obtain such reports.

Applicant's Signature _____

PRAIRIE LIGHTS BOOKS
15 South Dubuque St.
IOWA CITY, IOWA 52240
1 (319)337-2681

*Prospective employees
will receive consideration
without discrimination because
of race, creed, color, sex, age,
national origin or handicap.*

APPLICATION FOR EMPLOYMENT

PERSONAL

Last Name First Middle	Date
Street Address	Home Phone ( ) -
City, State, Zip	Business Phone ( ) -
Have you ever applied for employment with us? ☐Yes ☐No If Yes: Month and Year _____ Location _____	Social Security No.
Position Desired	Pay Expected
Apart from absence for religious observance, are you available for full-time work? ☐ Yes ☐No If not, what hours can you work? _____	Will you work overtime if asked? ☐ Yes ☐ No
Are you legally eligible for employment in the United States?	When will you available to begin work?
Other special training or skills (languages, machine operation, etc.)	

WORK EXPERIENCE

Company Name	Telephone ( ) -
Address	Employed (State Month and Year) From To
Name of Supervisor	Weekly Pay Start Last
State Job Title and Describe Your Work	Reason for Leaving

Company Name	Telephone ( ) -
Address	Employed (State Month and Year) From To
Name of Supervisor	Weekly Pay Start Last
State Job Title and Describe Your Work	Reason for Leaving

EDUCATIONAL EXPERIENCE

SCHOOL	NAME AND LOCATION OF SCHOOL	COURSE OF STUDY	NO. OF YEARS COMPLETED	DID YOU GRADUATE?	DEGREE OR DIPLOMA
College				☐ Yes ☐ No	
High				☐ Yes ☐ No	
Elementary				☐ Yes ☐ No	
Other				☐ Yes ☐ No	

In your own handwriting, list your ten favorite books and/or authors.

Part III

THE INTERVIEW

BE
PREPARED

For most of you, a job interview is not a completely new experience. You've been there before. You've had good interviews, you've had bad interviews, and you've had others that fell somewhere in between.

Some interviews seemed more like an interrogation or a court-martial; others were so informal you left feeling as if you had had a friendly chat with an old pal. Interviewing is not predictable, but it might help to think of going to an interview as something like going on a blind date. It's hard to know what to expect. The first few minutes are bound to be a bit awkward; you're not sure what you'll find to talk about or if you'll have anything in common.

You're about to meet a stranger whom you may never see again or who could possibly play a very important part in your life. You want to make a good impression, so you think about what you're going to wear, what you might want to talk about, and you think about some of the things you want to find out. Getting ready for an interview requires the same kind of effort.

Lack of preparation is the biggest pitfall for job seekers of any age. It's unwise to depend on inspiration to carry you through the interview. Before you can consider yourself ready to meet a potential employer, you have to know what you're getting into, something about the employer, and a great deal about yourself.

Will the Job Be Right for You?

Not all questions are asked in the interview room. There are some you must ask yourself long before you meet an employer. For example, you have to know how much time you can commit to a job. How many hours can you work? Can you consider part-time work or do you need a full 40-hour week? Can you work overtime or be on call for additional hours? Can you work days only? Evening hours? Night shift? Rotating shifts? If necessary, could you work consecutive shifts? Can you be away from home overnight—or for days at a time—if the job requires travel?

There are other questions, too. Can you tolerate the working conditions (noise, dust, chemicals)? Can you stand or sit for the standard working day? Are you allergic to the company's product? Are you philosophically or morally opposed to their objectives?

These are not simple questions, nor should they be answered "on the spot" without advance thought. Thinking ahead can help you avoid wasting time and energy applying for jobs that aren't for you.

Know Your Employer

Before you show up for an interview, you need to know something about the employer. At the most basic level, that means you need to know what they do.

▼ Do they manufacture a product?

▼ Do they sell that product? Or ship it out for someone else to sell?

▼ Do they work directly with clients?

▼ Do they provide a service?

▼ Are they independently owned? Or part of a chain?

Finding answers to these questions does not require extensive research. It's much easier than that. Pick up your telephone. Call your contacts to inquire if they know anything about the employer or if they can refer you to someone more knowledgeable. Better yet, call the company directly. The person who answers the phone can probably give you all the answers you need. And you don't even have to identify yourself.

You could spend hours digging out this information in your public library or from the chamber of commerce of small business associations. If it's a large company, you could spend an inordinate amount of time reading financial statements, balance sheets, projections, growth charts, and any number of promotional brochures available to stockholders and the general public. For some jobs, this  type of research is helpful and worth the hours it takes. But for many jobs, *some knowledge* is all that is required. Don't waste time gathering information you don't need; use the time to search for other job leads and to work on your interview skills.

What Kind of Interview?

There are two primary types of interviews, each with a distinct purpose. Screening interviews are usually conducted by a recruiter or personnel specialist. As the name implies, the screening process is designed to eliminate all but the most qualified applicants. Those who survive the screening interview will more than likely be called back for a second round. The second interview, the selection interview, will usually give you the opportunity to meet the person for whom you will work.

In a screening interview, you are likely to meet just one person. A selection interview can involve a series of people or even a team of interviewers. Often the type of job determines the complexity of the selection process. The point is, whatever type of interview you encounter, you must be prepared, adaptable, and flexible.

Impressing the Interviewer

How employers make the final selection to fill a position may be something of a mystery, but what they look for is not. Research studies about how people get hired all boil down to a few basics that contribute to making a positive impression.

To improve your chances of getting hired:

BE INFORMED

Know something about the employer. Read any literature available, do your homework, and be prepared to show how you fit in.

BE ON TIME

Arriving too early can cause waiting-room jitters. But there is no such thing as being fashionably late for an interview.

BE INDEPENDENT

Family members and friends do not belong at your interview. Go alone. Don't apply with a friend. Job hunting in pairs can cut your chances in half.

BE COURTEOUS

The interviewer is not the only one who should be impressed by your manner. Receptionists are important, too, and their opinions may count.

BE ALERT

Don't get so wrapped up in yourself that you lose track of what's going on. Pay attention to the interviewer. A good listener is a rare commodity.

BE SERIOUS

Wit is always an asset, but you're not here to entertain. If any jokes are told, let them come from the interviewer. Save yours for happy hour.

BE POSITIVE

Nobody wants to hire a complainer, a whiner, or a loser. Grumbling about the weather, the traffic, or about previous employers makes it easy for the interviewer to tune you out.

AND, OF COURSE, BE APPROPRIATELY DRESSED

Appearance can never be discounted. Looking good from head to toe will always improve your chances of getting hired.

LOOK
THE PART

Knowing what the company does is important, but knowing how the employees dress can help you to look as if you belong there. If you have the chance, case the place. Walk in and casually look around. Notice what people are wearing. Your observations can help you avoid arriving at an interview inappropriately under-dressed or overdressed.

If you cannot visit the company in advance, find a comparable one. You can find similar kinds of workplaces in your own community. Let's face it: a bank is a bank; one insurance company is much like another.

If you have any doubt about your interview clothing, a good—and safe—rule is to dress just a little better than you would expect to dress on the job. Choosing your interview outfit is an important decision. Don't just throw on whatever's handy.

MAKE SURE IT LOOKS GOOD ON YOU, MAKE SURE YOU FEEL COMFORTABLE IN IT, AND MAKE SURE IT BLENDS IN WITH THE WORK SETTING.

> *Jane Murrow applied for a position as a bank teller. Although she is 52 and hasn't worked outside the home for many years, she has recently taken courses in bookkeeping, word processing and, for her own enjoyment, a class in birdwatching.*
>
> *Jane arranged an interview by telephone and felt good about going in to meet the personnel director. She arrived at the interview punctually, did not feel intimidated, talked easily with the interviewer, and left with the feeling that she had a pretty good chance at the position. She was deeply disappointed to learn, two days later, that someone else had been selected.*

What went wrong?

Dale Carlson, the personnel director, saw it this way. Jane was competent to perform the duties of the job, and there was no question about her ability to handle money or keep records. However, the image Jane projected did not coincide with the bank's desired image. Why?

Even though Dale and Jane are about the same age, when she walked into his office, he felt he was receiving a visitor from out of the past. Jane's polyester pantsuit looked totally out of fashion, both in fabric and design. But what really convinced Dale that she would not fit in was her more-than-occasional use of "Super!" and her references to "the other girls" in the office.

Dale could not take a chance on someone who seemed out of touch with contemporary fashion and current modes of expression and who seemed to have an old-fashioned,

sexist attitude toward hiring patterns and staff roles.

The woman Dale hired stepped into the job, learned the routines easily, and was quickly accepted by her co-workers, Rollie, Janet, and Marie.

She was 53.

Image

It's OK to look your age. But it's not OK to look as if time has passed you by. Jane Murrow's mistake was in projecting an image that made it difficult to see her as contemporary.

The easiest item to deal with is your appearance. Selecting appropriate interview clothing depends upon the type of job you are seeking.

But be sure your choice is comparable to what today's workers are wearing.

This does not mean trendy, and it need not mean expensive.

It does mean you have to look as if you will fit in with your colleagues. You must look as though you belong in the workplace.

Fashions are changeable and often of short duration. They vary from one location to another; what's fashionable in San Francisco may look quite different in Wichita.

Images are consistent but not static.

Before you even have the chance to open your mouth to say hello, you've made a statement about yourself. Your image is already working for you or against you. It's not possible to please everyone, but you can concentrate on not offending anyone. For any interview, these items are **OUT**:

✗ plunging necklines

✗ filmy blouses

✗ skintight tops (or bottoms)

✗ the "evening look"

✗ extreme hemlines

✗ jeans

✗ outdated or ultramodern hairstyles

✗ excessive jewelry (nothing dangling, glittery, noisy, or feathered)

✗ medals or badges that denote fraternal or religious affiliations

✗ strong perfume, after-shave, cologne

✗ heavy or exotic makeup

✗ scuffed shoes (don't even consider hunting boots, sneakers, sandals, or moccasins)

✗ unusually long fingernails

✗ chipped nail polish

✗ sunglasses (put them in your pocket or purse, not on your face)

✗ tattoos (cover them)

✗ purses (if you're also carrying a briefcase or portfolio, one bag is all you're allowed)

✗ loud colors, unusual patterns

✗ hats (you can wear a hat to—but not during—an interview)

✗ both suspenders and belts (choose one or the other)

And

✗ cigarettes

✗ chewing gum or breath mints

✗ traces of food or alcohol on your breath

Head First

Grooming is just as important as attire. There are never any exceptions to the basics of good grooming, but it is not enough just to be neat and clean. Start by taking a good look at yourself—and start at the top.

Is your hair attractively and appropriately styled? Make a point of telling your hairdresser you're applying for jobs and you need to look your best. Take a color check. Are you worried about your gray hair? If it's becoming to you and you're comfortable with it, leave it alone. If it makes you feel tired and old, do something about it. Turning brittle blonde or glossy black overnight is not the answer. Today, hair color can be a matter of choice, and you can still look natural.

This Applies to Men, Too!

And guys, keep reading . . .

The rest of this section is especially for you. You have special considerations regarding hair—or its absence. "Bald is beautiful" has real meaning. It is always preferable to ill-fitting or ill-matched cover-ups.

If you are going to invest in a hairpiece, you must be willing to spend the money it takes to get a good one. Nothing is more ridiculous than a shag rug atop your head.

While we're on the subject of hair loss, there is nothing to be gained by parting your hair just over one ear and sweeping the few remaining strands across. This technique never fooled anyone and only accentuates the condition.

Facial hair remains a controversial issue. As a general rule, beards are fine for centennial celebrations, but they do not match the corporate image of most businesses.

Shaving off a beard you've grown accustomed to can be a difficult decision—even a traumatic event—but it may be in your best interest. Before you take the plunge, however, consider the kind of job you want and the expected standard of your potential employers.

If you feel you look better with a beard and you decide to take your chances with a hairy face, be sure it is neatly trimmed. A professional's advice and assistance can help you shape your beard to the most becoming style for you.

A mustache is not usually a barrier to employment even with conservative employers. But the same rules for neatness and style apply.

Sideburns, on the other hand, must follow current fashion trends.

Pay particular attention to other unsightly hair. Eyebrows may need trimming; hairs protruding from the nose or ears must be attended to. People do notice. People do make hiring judgments based on appearance.

A few minor grooming techniques might make a difference in how others see you—and even in how you see yourself.

STRESS
STRESS
STRESS
STRESS

Your dictionary will tell you that stress is a force exerted upon a body. When that body is yours, you know what your symptoms are. Under stress, people sweat, giggle, twitch, fidget, stammer, blush, turn pale, tremble, or become disoriented. Some lose sleep. Some lose their appetite; others can't stop eating. Some start smoking more—or again. Some get ulcers; others get irritable. Some rush for the bathroom. Others head for the nearest bar.

A little nervousness is natural. Employers expect it, they're not bothered by it, and you shouldn't be, either. In fact, being a little on edge will probably help you to be more energetic, enthusiastic, and competitive. Adrenalin is a valuable commodity; welcome it and use it to your advantage.

STRESS

Only a fool would tell you that looking for a job isn't stressful. And it would take an even bigger fool to tell you that interviews will not produce stress. After all, you're in an unfamiliar setting, meeting strangers, risking your ego, and about to embark on a conversation that can affect the rest of your life.

What Do You Do about Stress?

First, accept it. Denying that stress exists is pointless and can be hazardous to your working life. Better to recognize it, plan for it, and learn how to cope with it. The last thing you need is a panic attack during your interview. Above all, don't let stress force you into trying to be someone you're not. Some people try to overcompensate by assuming a Superman or Wonderwoman facade. Others are intimidated and wilt.

You may not be able to control your feelings, but you can keep your feelings from controlling the interview.

Your body has a tendency to let the employer know how you feel. You can improve your interview image by using a few simple techniques to make yourself appear relaxed and confident in spite of what's happening inside.

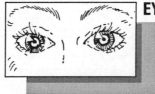

EYE CONTACT

It all starts here. We establish communication by meeting each other's gaze.

If you have trouble looking the employer in the eye, you're going to appear insecure, aloof, or troubled. There is a way to get around it: look at the bridge of the nose or pretend you're reading the interviewer's lips.

They'll never know the difference.

CAUTION: Don't overdo it. Staring is just as bad as avoidance. Eye contact should be frequently interrupted and naturally reestablished. It's perfectly acceptable to let your gaze wander while you are talking, but, at the end of your response, try to catch the interviewer's eye to signal that you have made your point.

SHAKING HANDS

A handshake is an integral part of an introduction. Have your hand ready; don't be caught off guard. If you tend to have sweaty palms, have a tissue ready for a last-minute swipe before you go in. Then forget about it.

Your handshake communicates something about you, so make yours count. A firm clasp is acceptable. An overenergetic vicelike hold, vigorous pumping, or an extended, lingering grip will not win you any points, and limp, lifeless paws are simply awful. Handshakes are nonsexist and old social rules no longer apply;

women or men should feel free to initiate a handshake and should always be prepared to reciprocate.

FOREIGN OBJECTS (BUSY FINGERS SYNDROME)

Men, leave your change at home. You don't want to sound like a walking piggy-bank, nor do you want to risk distracting yourself and the interviewer by jingling the coins in your pocket while you are talking.

Women, put your handbag on the floor, not on your lap. And whether you're a man or a woman, do not twirl a ring, play with a pen, or pick up anything from the interviewer's desk.

SIT UP

Don't settle into the chair as if you were relaxing at home in front of the TV. If you keep away from the back of the chair, your posture will be better, you won't have to worry about crossing your legs, and your hands will naturally stay in your lap.

Note: Hard chairs are always preferable to overstuffed chairs or couches. If you have a choice, be sure to select a chair that allows you to sit upright. You'll look more alert, you'll be less likely to slouch, and you won't have to be concerned about your arms and hands.

> *You don't need to look as if you were having tea with the Queen, but you do want to appear poised and attentive.*

WATCH YOUR BODY LANGUAGE Trying to hide your hands, crossing your arms in front of your chest, putting your hands in your pockets, or resting your chin in your hand will detract from your image.

Beware of the power pose: arms raised, elbows out, fingers interlocked behind your head. Bosses can act this way during a board meeting. Job seekers can't get away with it.

Try all of these attitudes in front of a mirror at home. Your mirror will show you what happens.

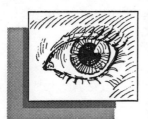

KEEP YOUR EYES OPEN

Interviewers give nonverbal cues, too, especially when they're ready to draw the interview to a close. Be on the lookout for signals. If the interviewer seems to lose concentration, switches eye contact away from you to other objects in the room, shuffles papers, or pushes back from the desk, you can be fairly certain it's time to go. Finish what you're saying, but don't prolong the conversation.

MAKE A GRACEFUL EXIT

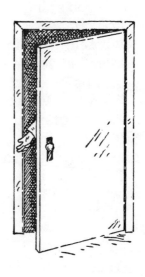

Once the interview is over, keep your composure at least until you're outside the door. Don't ruin a good first impression by rushing through the final stage. Show as much confidence as you did when you arrived. Smile, thank the interviewer for the opportunity to discuss the position, and don't leave anything but a good feeling behind you.

Mirror, Mirror, on the Wall . . .

Check Yourself

Your mirror doesn't have to tell you that you are the fairest in all the land. But look into it, anyway. It can tell you some things you need to know. Don't just use the mirror to tell you if your tie is crooked or your slip is showing. Look a little deeper.

Enlist the help of a full-length mirror. If you don't have one, spend a few bucks. It will be one of the best investments you can make when you're looking for a job.

Set it up and go to work.

Stand in front of it. Check out your posture. Are your shoulders drooping? Is your chin up? Are your hands relaxed, or are they hanging there like a bunch of bananas? Do you look fresh? Or do you look like you've just run a marathon? Do you need a haircut, a new style, or a highlight? Does your interview outfit compliment your figure? Is the color right for you? Look down—are your shoes polished?

Don't walk away from your mirror just yet. Pull up a chair and sit down. Better yet, sit up. Take another look.

Are you sitting forward in your chair?

Do your hands look relaxed and comfortable?

Women: How does your skirt look from this angle?

Men: Did you remember to unbutton your jacket, or is it bunched around your middle?

Everyone: Where are your feet?

Finally, are you smiling?

If your mirror doesn't reflect a smile, do something about it right this minute.

Put on a smile, and look at the difference.

You'll look better,
you'll feel better,
and you'll sound better.

You're never dressed for an interview without a smile.

SOUND THE PART

Once you're satisfied with your appearance, you can move on to another aspect of your image—your voice. Unless you've worked as a talk-show host or a radio commentator, you probably haven't had much of a chance to listen to yourself, to evaluate how you sound to others.

Listen to Yourself

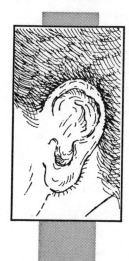

Is your voice overpowering? If so, you might need to turn the volume down a bit. Or do you sound timid and frail? Speak up! Your story is too important to be lost in a whisper.

Do you sound cheerful? Alert? Friendly? If you sound discouraged, dull, or hostile, that's the impression you're going to leave with the employer. Your manner of speaking can outweigh the content of your responses; you don't want the interviewer to remember you as the one who sounded tired, crabby, or bored.

The quality of your voice can make a big difference in the overall impression you'll make on an employer. Interview jitters and anxieties can play tricks; many people respond to stress by raising the pitch of their voice. With a little conscious effort, you can lower your voice and avoid sounding nervous or tense.

Pronounce your words carefully. Don't drop the ends of your words or fade out as you near the end of a sentence. Take a deep breath and answer with confidence. Listen to the rate of your speech. Do . . . you . . . talk . . . too . . . slowly? Or do you talksofastitishardtounderstand-whatyouaresaying? Again, be aware that tension can increase your rate of speech.

A dull, plodding, monotonous tone makes you sound as if you would be a dull, plodding worker. Put some energy and enthusiasm in your voice; you'll sound capable and ambitious.

A tape recorder can help you do a spot-check of your vocal image, and you can do it in complete privacy. Turn on the tape recorder and introduce yourself. Then say something about your skills, and respond to this question: "What was the best job you ever had, and why?"

Rewind the tape, switch it on, and listen to yourself. That voice may sound like it's coming from a stranger, but it's really you. That's how you sound to others. Play it back as many times as you need to in order to check

✓ *diction,*

✓ *tone,*

✓ *pitch,*

✓ *energy level,*

✓ *confidence, and*

✓ *rate.*

In addition, a tape recorder can help you catch and correct a few other little habits and mannerisms: nervous laughter at the end of a sentence, excessive slang or jargon, and the various verbal tics that can creep into our conversation—"um, er, well, you know, OK, right."

Looking at yourself—
     listening to yourself—
          will pay off.

PRACTICE MAY NOT MAKE
YOU PERFECT
BUT IT WILL MAKE
YOU BETTER

The Right Word

Unless you're applying for a modeling job, you aren't going to be hired solely on the basis of your appearance. What you say and how you say it will make a difference. All experts agree—

How You Talk
     tells the employer
          How You Think.

Your ability to communicate can signal that you are a viable worker, or it can alert the employer that you are trying to relive your youth, coasting toward retirement, or otherwise out of touch.

Use Proper Grammar

If you've forgotten the rules Miss Jones taught you in grammar class back in eighth grade, brush up now before it's too late. Do yourself and your interviewer a favor, and

DON'T SAY	**DO SAY**
theirselves	*themselves*
ain't	*am not, isn't, or aren't*
I done	*I did*
can't hardly	*can hardly*
I come yesterday	*I came yesterday*
She don't	*She doesn't*
If I was	*If I were*
I been	*I have been*
Between you and I	*Between you and me*
He's left	*He's gone*

These common mistakes can hurt you. Catch them and correct them.

Check Your Pronunciation

Be sure you can properly pronounce the words you choose. It's never too late to break old habits. You'd be surprised how many people will pick up on minor mispronunciations. Some of the most common errors are:

Febuary for February

Warshington for Washington

Pitcher for Picture

Libary for Library

Accidently for Accidentally

Often for Often (the *t* is silent)

Athalete for Athlete

Eye-talian for Italian

Relator for Realtor

Oncet for Once

Excape for Escape

Watch Out for Slang

Your conversation doesn't have to be formal or stilted, but you shouldn't sound like a teen-ager in disguise, either. Use slang very sparingly. Overuse of contemporary slang gives the impression you're trying to be younger than your chronological age. However, clinging to phrases, expressions, or words that were popular back when you were going to proms makes you look like you never grew up.

Cut the # + * @ !

Profanity, although it has gained acceptance and even popularity in the media, can never help you make a good impression on an employer. Even if the interviewer should reel off a string of four-letter words, don't follow suit. For all you know, the interviewer is testing you. Take no chances.

Don't Sound Dated

And for those of you who are pushing 50—or dragging it behind you—avoid these

Old-Timer's Phrases

At my age . . .
When I was starting out . . .
Back then . . .
The boys I worked with . . .
The lady at the front desk . . .
When I was younger . . .
Years ago . . .
At my prime . . .
I used to be able to . . .
When you're my age . . .
I remember when . . .
I always used to . . .
People my age . . .
The girls in the office . . .
In the old days . . .
Right after the war . . .
Let me tell you, young man . . .
She's a good ol' gal . . .

These phrases all look back. Today they sound sexist, trite, or unimaginative—and some of them were pretty bad even then. Go through your inventory of words and phrases, and clean out the cobwebs.

Think carefully before you speak so that you do not fall back on any of these expressions.

ONCE UPON A TIME... Children are fascinated with these words. Employers are not. Old-timers have the reputation of being storytellers. They talk and talk and talk. That's another reason to avoid these phrases; many of them sound like the introduction to a long, rambling narrative. They are tired, old clichés, and they take the energy out of the point you are trying to make. Drop them. Practice being clear and concise. *Don't be a storyteller.*

The Past Is Prologue

Dwelling on the past when you are talking to an employer is sure to keep you from having a future with that company. Your past is part of you, and you will want to share with an interviewer some of your previous work experiences and accomplishments. But don't overwhelm the listener with history. Focus on your skills, your abilities, and your eagerness to perform the duties of the new job now and in the future.

No Apologies, No Excuses

Don't get caught up in apologizing for what you have failed to accomplish. Some things you can't change. You can't change your chronological age, nor can you change past events. Everything that has ever happened to you, everything that you have ever done, has served to make you what you are today.

That person—
your present self—
is what you have to deal with.

Don't think you have to make excuses for your present situation. Many people say, "If only I had my life to live over again, I would do things differently." Whether we would indeed do things differently is something we'll never have the chance to find out. Given the chance, most of us probably would not choose to relive our pasts.

R.I.P. Chivalry

Chivalry is, finally, dead. And in the business world it is unlamented. It has been replaced by simple good manners. The distinction between men and women—at least in the work force—is gone. A man does not have to wait for a woman to initiate a handshake, nor should he rush to open a door for a female counterpart nor leap to his feet each time a woman enters the room. Rules governing social situations do not apply at work, and the code of manners you were taught as a child will have to give way to contemporary practices.

Drill sergeants may still demand a "Yes, Sir!" In any other situation, it is no longer necessary or even appropriate to tack "Sir" or "Ma'am" onto the end of each sentence you utter.

Note: there are exceptions to every rule, and regional customs should be followed. Southerners, for example, still maintain frequent use of "Sir" and "Ma'am." This usage remains very much a part of their business and social lives.

If you are relocating, pay attention to local customs.

IMAGE CHECK ✔

My interview outfit, from head to toe, will be:

Clothing: _____

_____

_____

Shoes: _____
Accessories: _____

_____

_____

Hair Check: _____Cut _____Style _____Color

_____Beard/Mustache _____Trim

I need to
work on: A. Old-timer phrases

B. Storytelling

C. Updating my manners

D. All of the above

On a scale of 1 to 10, my image as a job seeker is:

1 2 3 4 5 6 7 8 9 10

ON YOUR WAY

1. Be prepared.

2. Know where you're going.

3. Allow plenty of time.

4. And always go alone.

These could be considered the four cardinal rules for interview success. They may seem obvious—and they are—but many employers will tell you they're not followed very carefully.

An applicant who is obviously prepared and organized is already well on the way to making a good impression. Take a little time to pull together the following items:

Interview Kit

✓ several copies of your resume
✓ a list of references (with addresses and phone numbers)
✓ letters of recommendation
✓ social security card
✓ a good pen

You might not need all of them at any one interview, but you'll look good if you can produce these items when they are required.

Don't leave home without some extra cash in your wallet or purse. Getting caught empty-handed can be embarrassing or worse. There's always the chance you might have a flat tire, an unexpected cab fare, or even a luncheon expense.

Tuck a lucky charm in your billfold, too. Not a rabbit's foot, just a small piece of paper with the five words you have chosen to describe yourself (page 17). Just knowing it's there will make it easier to remember these words and work them into your interview conversation.

There's enough stress and tension involved in interviewing without complicating the process by running late, getting lost, or being held up in traffic. You don't need back-seat drivers, either.

Allow plenty of time to get where you're going, with a few extra minutes to freshen up and catch your breath.

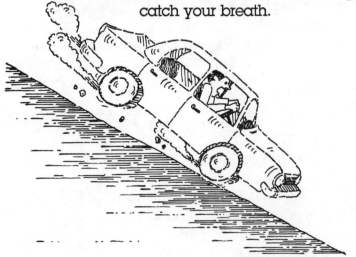

> *Wendy's Waiting Room Woes began when she arrived more than an hour early for a 9:45 appointment. First of all, the office wasn't even open yet. When the receptionist arrived, there stood Wendy outside the door. Her first impression was already shaky. Wendy found herself sitting in the waiting room for nearly an hour. As other applicants arrived, she tried to strike up conversations, and she frequently interrupted the receptionist with comments about the weather, the traffic, even questions about the boss. With 30 minutes to go, she decided to finish knitting the sleeve of a sweater. When the time finally came for her interview, Wendy thought it went very well—and it did. She was articulate, enthusiastic, and able to demonstrate excellent skills and a real interest in the job. But when the interviewer asked the receptionist for her impressions, it was all over for Wendy.*

The waiting room should not be an obstacle in your job search, and the less time you spend there, the less likely it will be a problem. Plan to arrive about ten minutes before a scheduled appointment. Introduce yourself to the receptionist, hang your coat (if possible) so that you won't have to lug it with you, find a comfortable place to sit, and spend the little time you have left thinking about questions you might want to raise and responses you want to give. Keep your conversation to a minimum, be ready when your name is called, and be prepared for an introductory handshake.

THE HEART OF THE MATTER

It is impossible to overestimate the importance of the first few minutes of an interview. It's probably not true, though you might have heard it, that the decision to hire is made in the first couple of minutes. More likely the decision *not* to hire is made that early. It's very difficult to overcome a negative first impression.

THE 4-SECOND SMILE

❏ Smile.

❏ Make eye contact.

❏ Say your name.

❏ Shake hands.

❏ You should still be smiling.

In the four seconds that have just gone by, you have made a strong statement about yourself.

If you practice these four seconds until you can introduce yourself naturally and without hesitation, you will never have to worry about getting off on the wrong foot and you'll never have to try to salvage a poor introduction. You can get on with the interview feeling poised and confident.

Beyond the First Impression

Once you've passed the critical first-impression test, you have the opportunity to demonstrate, through your responses, that you have something to contribute, that you have the qualities and skills the employer needs.

Not all jobs are alike. Specific jobs require specific skills. The interviewer might be looking for a secretary who can take dictation at a minimum rate of 120 words per minute, a mechanic who knows German-made motors inside and out, or a computer programmer with experience in both COBOL and FORTRAN. Such qualities are easily assessed. Either you have them or you don't, and you won't be hired without them. But skills alone may not land the job for you.

Employers want to hire someone who can handle the responsibilities of the job, and they also want to hire someone who will

→ *Show up,*
  → *Take directions,*
  → *Follow through,*
    → *Get along with others,*
      → *Take responsibility, and*
      → *Communicate.*

You have to demonstrate through your responses and comments that you are—or will be—the kind of worker who exhibits these qualities.

After the preliminaries, and maybe after a few casual comments about anything from the weather to local sports, the interview should get down to its real purpose—the exchange of information. (To find out what to do if it doesn't, turn to "Rescuing an Interview," page 154.)

Though it's sometimes hard to realize, you are not in an inferior or subordinate position during an interview. Once you are hired, this person may be your boss, but that hasn't happened yet. Until it does, you and the interviewer are equal partners. Each of you should be ready and willing to

→ *ask questions,*
  → *listen carefully, and*
    → *give information.*

There can always be surprises. That's one reason interviewing can be interesting, challenging, maybe even fun. But if you think about it, you'll realize that employers are going to be interested in three basic things:

→ *what you've done,*
  → *what you're prepared to do,*
    → *and what skills and qualities you can bring to the job.*

To get this information, most employers will ask some of the following 50 questions in one form or another.

50 QUESTIONS ASKED BY EMPLOYERS

1. Tell me about yourself.
2. Why should we hire you?
3. What did you dislike most about your previous boss/ supervisor?
4. What do you know about our company?
5. Why do you want to work here?
6. What are your short-range/long-range goals?
7. Why are you changing jobs?
8. What do you look for in an ideal job?
9. Are you looking for a permanent or temporary job?
10. What two or three things are most important to you in your job?
11. Are you self-motivated? Organized?
12. How do you work in a group?

13. What did you like about your previous job?

14. How do you work under stress, pressure, and deadlines?

15. What work do you enjoy the most? Least?

16. What are your strengths? Weaknesses?

17. Name three major accomplishments in your present job.

18. What qualifications do you have for this job?

19. How would you evaluate your performance on your present job?

20. What have you learned from your mistakes?

21. How do you think your education has prepared you for this job?

22. Are you more comfortable working by yourself or with others?

23. Tell me about a problem you have solved in your present job.

24. Have you had experience as a supervisor? In what capacity?

25. What salary do you expect?

26. What has influenced your career decisions?

27. Do you object to overtime? Travel? Rotating shifts?

28. What interests you about this type of work?

29. Have you had any experience in this line of work?

30. Tell me about someone you admire.

31. When you were in school, what courses did you like best? Least?

32. Give me three adjectives that describe you.

33. How would your supervisor describe you?

34. What do you like to do in your spare time?

35. What would you do if a dissatisfied customer started shouting at you about a defective product?

36. What types of books have you read lately?

37. Have you taken any classes recently? Attended workshops/seminars?

38. Define success.

39. Would you be willing to relocate?

40. Give me a specific example of something you've done that shows initiative.

41. What person has had the greatest influence on you?

42. Tell me about your past attendance record. What do you consider an acceptable attendance record?

43. Describe a good supervisor.

44. What did you earn on previous jobs?

45. What can you tell me about your current job?

46. Why do you want to start working again?

47. What do you see yourself doing in five years?

48. What community activities have you been involved in?

49. Is there anything else I should know?

50. What questions do you have for me?

Because you can anticipate encountering these questions (and more), you can help yourself by thinking about your responses in advance of the interview. (For questions about salary history and expected salary, see

"Paychecks and Priorities," pages 163–168.) Let's take a look at the first three questions, which illustrate different types of open-ended questions.

1. Tell me about yourself.

This is a difficult question to interpret, but it's a very popular question with both inexperienced and highly skilled interviewers. Some interviewers might pose this question simply to break the ice, to get you to talk a bit about yourself. Experienced interviewers are more likely to use this question to make an important evaluation. You won't always be able to tell why your interviewer asks this question, but that doesn't matter; your response should be the same whatever the interviewer's motive.

The best response is one that promotes your skills, your qualifications, and your personality. Do not—repeat, Do Not—give an autobiographical sketch. Talking about your parents, your childhood, the schools you attended, your marital status, your children, and your favorite hobbies will tell the interviewer you're probably not the person for the job.

Simply repeating facts and dates regarding your education and employment history is not a good idea, either. It's redundant; the interviewer probably has this information on your resume and application form.

> **THE KEY TO ANSWERING "TELL ME ABOUT YOURSELF" QUESTIONS IS TO CONCENTRATE ON YOUR SKILLS AND ATTRIBUTES.**

Because this question comes up so frequently, you should take the time to think about your response. Plan to use the five words you chose to describe yourself. Work them in along with a couple of specific illustrations. Most applicants will lose the interviewer's attention with unnecessary and irrelevant information. You can make the question work for you.

2. Why Should We Hire You?

Many applicants are uncomfortable with this question because they feel they have to blow their own horns. Instead of dreading it, you should look forward to it. You don't have to claim to be better than your competitors, and you don't have to brag. All you have to do is let the interviewer know, in a short, enthusiastic statement, that you have the background, the motivation, and the interest to succeed in the job.

> THOSE WHO BEG FOR A JOB, WHO TALK ABOUT BEING BROKE, HAVING THEIR CAR REPOSSESSED, OR BEING BEHIND ON MORTGAGE PAYMENTS MAY ELICIT SYMPATHY BUT NOT A JOB. JOBS GO TO PEOPLE WHO HAVE SOMETHING TO OFFER.

3. What Did You Dislike about Your Previous Boss/Supervisor?

It doesn't matter if you worked for Attila the Hun; this is not the time to tell horror stories. You don't have to lie, either. But you can tell the truth in a positive light.

> *Steve has been working for a worka-holic tyrant for the past four years. His boss is unable to delegate authority or to believe that anyone could carry through a project without his direct day-to-day involvement. Most annoying is the boss's habit of commenting only about small details he would have handled differently. No praise or even acceptance is ever shown.*
>
> *Steve knows it would be interview suicide to share these things, so he answered the question this way: "My boss is very precise and very attentive to detail. He's demanding and, consequently, I've learned a lot from him. If I have any criticism, it's that I sometimes feel I could be even more effective if I could be more independent. I know I could solve my own problems."*

Rescuing an Interview

A skilled professional interviewer can help you feel comfortable, make it easy for you to respond, and still gather all the information needed to evaluate your strengths and skills.

Enjoy these interviews because there just aren't enough good interviewers to go around.

Unfortunately for applicants, not everyone involved in the hiring process is a good interviewer. You're likely to meet a number of amateurs. Some will be rookies for life, others will learn on the job.

In their defense, many don't want to be there. Some interviewers are there by default: there's no one else to do it, they have been drafted under protest, or company policy requires them to participate in the selection process. If you're lucky, reluctant interviewers will have a standard set of questions for all applicants, but it's just as likely the interview will have no set pattern and will be thirty minutes of off-the-cuff remarks and impromptu questions.

Under these circumstances, a half-hour can seem an eternity—both for you and the interviewer. It's not unusual for interviewers to break the ice by asking about the weather, sports, or other topics of local interest. This is fine, but it will work against you if it lasts more than five minutes.

This is where your preparation can pay off. If you know who you are and what you can do, there's bound to be some point in the interview where you can steer the conversation toward your skills and strengths. You can't wait for the interviewer to get around to asking about them. You have to take control. Unless you do, your chances of getting hired are slim.

After the initial chitchat, the interviewer might proceed to tell you about the job, sometimes in great and terrible detail. Of course you want to know what you're getting into, but if the entire interview turns out to be a description of the duties and responsibilities of the job, you're basically what you were when the interview began—an unknown quantity.

TAKE A RISK

If you find yourself in this situation, you might have to do something you were taught never to do—interrupt. Look at it as survival. It's your job that's slipping away. If you don't find a way to promote your skills, you're not going to get hired.

Take a deep breath, plant your feet firmly on the floor, and speak up. You might say something like, "Excuse me. The job you're describing is very interesting to me because . . ." Then launch into a quick run-down of your skills that relate directly to this job. This tactic might not work every time, but it's worth the gamble.

Who's on the Other Side of the Desk?

Like job seekers, interviewers come in all sizes, shapes, colors, and ages. Some are kind, thoughtful, articulate, fair, and genuinely interested in you as a person. Others are gruff, inconsiderate, biased, and hurried. The majority fall somewhere in between, and, chances are, your interviews will expose you to all of these personality types and more.

Some interviewers are very well trained, knowledgeable about what they do, and even give you the feeling they enjoy talking with you. Often, these people are capable of conducting an in-depth interview without making you break out into a cold sweat. At the end of the interview you may feel you simply had a nice conversation.

Who Is This Kid?

One of the startling things about maturing is the realization that other people seem to get younger and younger. We tend to think of people in authority as being older than we are, and we're comfortable with authority figures who are older or at least our own age. It comes as something of a shock when we find a doctor, dentist, or lawyer who looks like a teen-ager.

Mature job seekers are often faced with a younger interviewer. If this happens to you, don't let it affect your interview performance. You don't want to be judged on the basis of your age—don't judge the interviewer, either. Assume the interviewer is competent and get on with the business at hand— discussing and promoting your qualifications for the job.

Inappropriate Questions

There are some questions you shouldn't be asked. Unfortunately, in spite of federal and state guidelines for pre-employment inquiries, chances are you'll encounter at least as many inappropriate or even illegal questions in interviews as you did on application forms.

Some employers ask these questions even though they know they are not appropriate. Others will ask them out of ignorance or naivete. It is quite possible, especially in a small business or a "mom and pop" operation, that some inappropriate questions may be raised innocently with no intent to discriminate. For example, an interviewer might think a question about your family will help you feel comfortable and make it easy for you to begin the conversation.

You don't have to try to figure out what the interviewer has in mind. In the first place, you don't have time, and second, you have a 50 percent chance of being wrong. Rather than trying to second-

20 QUESTIONS YOU SHOULDN'T BE ASKED

1. Do you wish to be addressed as Miss or Mrs.?
2. What is your spouse's occupation?
3. When and where were you born?
4. Do you mind answering some personal questions?
5. Whom should we notify in case of an emergency?
6. Where do your parents live and what do they do for a living?
7. What is your native tongue?
8. What is your marital status?
9. What is your religious affiliation?
10. How did you learn to read/write/speak a foreign language?
11. Have you ever been arrested?
12. Of what societies/clubs/lodges are you a member?
13. What type of military discharge did you receive?
14. Are you the principal wage earner of your household?
15. Do you have children?
16. Are you now pregnant?
17. Who cares for your children while you are at work?
18. Have you ever been treated for a mental or emotional problem?
19. Do you have a disability?
20. What was your maiden name?

guess the interviewer, it's a good idea to have thought
about these inappropriate questions and to have decided
how you will handle them.

What Are Your Options?

> *Ruth was interviewing for*
> *a staff nurse position in a*
> *small hospital. The inter-*
> *view began well, with a*
> *couple of minutes of small*
> *talk. Then she was asked*
> *about her marital status.*
> *This was a problem question*
> *for her. She was in the proc-*
> *ess of getting a divorce from*
> *her fourth husband, and she*
> *really didn't want the em-*
> *ployer to know about her*
> *marital record.*

There are several ways Ruth could handle this question. Because she felt that giving the information would
work against her, she could simply say she would provide information about marital status upon employment.
Another option would be to answer the question by saying, "I've been married, but I don't consider that relevant
to my qualifications for the job." She might answer with a
question such as, "Is this information required?" Or she
might simply say, "I prefer not to answer that question." If
she felt more comfortable answering the question, she
would only say, "I'm in the process of a divorce." Under
no circumstances is she obligated to elaborate or to introduce the topic of her other three husbands.

Make It a Two-Way Street

You should have some questions, too. It's very likely that at some point in the interview—often at the very end—the employer will ask if you have any questions. Two or three good questions can demonstrate your interest in the job, your awareness of how you can fit in, and could tip the scales in your favor.

Some of the following questions could be asked in nearly any interview situation. In addition, you may pick up a question or two in the course of your interview.

25 QUESTIONS YOU MIGHT ASK

1. What will be my duties in this position?

2. Is there a written job description?

3. What will be my principal responsibilities?

4. To whom do I report?

5. What type of training program will I be involved in?

6. When was this position created?

7. How many people have held this position?

8. How/by whom/how frequently will my work be evaluated?

9. How are promotions determined?

10. What is the salary range for this position?

11. Is the position considered entry-level? Mid-level?

12. Does the company post job listings for all openings within the organization?

13. How long do people usually stay in this job?

14. What is the typical working day/week?

15. What type of working environment will I have?

16. Will I share an office? Have my own?

17. May I see my work station?

18. What types of equipment/machines/systems will I be expected to use?

19. Is flextime available?

20. Will I be involved in evening or weekend business assignments?

21. Does the company have a physical fitness center? Employee counselor? Day-care center?

22. What type of job-related expenses could I expect?

23. Is there room for future advancement?

24. Does the company encourage/provide/fund continuing education for employees?

25. When do you expect to make a hiring decision?

No Further Questions

It can happen that the interviewer does such a good job of describing the position, the working conditions, and the compensation package, you really have all the information you need. If you find that you have no questions to ask, don't just sit there and shake your head no. Instead, you might say something like this: "You've answered all the questions I had, and I am very interested in the job. If I do think of something later, may I call you?"

Don't Talk Yourself Out of a Job

Saying too much is probably worse than saying too little. Keep your comments brief and on target.

> **Tammy Douglas was one of three finalists for an office manager's position in a large department. She handled the interview questions very well and was able to present favorable impressions about her supervisory and organizational skills, technical knowledge, and her ability to work with others. The director of the office was ready to make an offer but wanted Tammy to meet the assistant director who was not immediately available. In the ten minutes that followed, Tammy managed to talk herself out of a job. Uncomfortable with silence, she launched into a lengthy monologue about her favorite pastime, league softball. Much to the director's surprise, she proceeded to give a detailed account of the entire season. She hadn't yet reached the play-offs when the assistant director arrived, but by that time, she had struck out.**

Tammy's interview was great, but her introduction of a completely unrelated topic and her persistent chatter about outside interests were inappropriate and fatal. The interviewer was very pleased about the unexpected delay because Tammy's response to it indicated that she would probably bring the same kind of inappropriate behavior to the job. She wasn't hired.

Talktalktalk

Don't talk yourself out of a job. It's not your responsibility as an applicant to fill every silence—especially with chitchat. Never initiate conversation about unrelated topics, and don't dominate the conversation. Silence is far less harmful.

PAYCHECKS & PRIORITIES

It's tragic how many people lose out on jobs because they don't know how to talk about money. Some think they're worth more than they really are, others under-value their skills and their previous experiences, and still others are uninformed and naive about money matters.

Think back. Have you ever said,

"I'm cheap—just hire me."

"I'm worth $30,000, but I can start at $20,000."

"I can't remember what I made on my last job, but it wasn't much."

"I'm worth more than you're willing to pay."

"I don't know what I'm worth."

"Just give me a chance—we'll worry about money later."

"I know you have a reputation for not paying much, but . . ."

"I haven't worked for years—I'll take anything."

If you have said any of these things, chances are you didn't get hired. There's nothing to be gained from putting down the employer or yourself, as many of these comments do.

How Do I Deal with Money Matters?

The solution is easy. If an employer asks you either "What salary do you anticipate?" or "How much do you think you're worth?" you need to know one word: *negotiable*. If you're pressed further, ask what the salary range is for this particular position. Never give a dollar amount. If it's too high, you won't be considered. If it's too low, you may be stuck with it.

Don't get confused about salary history and salary range. If you're asked on an application form or during an interview about your salary history, the question is about dollar figures. Don't forget to add in the dollar value of your benefits package, and don't pin it down to the last penny. Tell the truth, but unless you're an accountant, you can probably get by with an approximate figure; round it off to the nearest hundred.

A salary range is a sliding scale and will include both the minimum and maximum amounts for the particular position or classification. The employer might have the flexibility to hire at any point within that range, and you may be able to negotiate a specific salary by indicating that you would probably fit into the middle or upper limits of the range. If you don't have relevant experience, you will likely be hired at the minimum figure; if you do have experience, you can try to negotiate for more money.

When to Talk about Money

The time to negotiate is once you've been offered a job; not at an interview—that's premature and presumptuous. At an interview, all you need to establish is that the job will or will not meet your needs and expectations.

You may not have to ask about money. The best employers will bring up the topic and tell you what you need to know. They may not get around to salary and benefits until quite late in the interview, however. Give them a chance; don't introduce the topic early, and don't appear more interested in the money than in the job.

If the interview is drawing to a close and the subject of compensation has not been raised, you should not hesitate to inquire. Smart job seekers often try this tactic first: "I've learned a great deal about the job and I'm very interested. Can you tell me about your benefit package?" Some employers offer only wages; others may have a smorgasbord of fringe benefits.

FRINGE BENEFITS

Insurance Policies

Health:	Employees eligible for group plan: all or part of premium may be paid by employer.
Dental/Vision:	Full or partial coverage for routine procedures.
Disability:	Partial compensation for employees unable to work.
Life:	Employer pays all or part of premium; additional coverage available at low group rate.
Sick Leave:	Set number of days per month of year.
Holidays:	Paid leave for specified days.
Vacation:	Annual leave with number of days usually determined by longevity.
Child Care:	Company provides facilities or helps defray cost of child care.
Savings Plan or Stock Option:	Employer matches all or part of employee savings or offers stock at less than market value.
Profit Sharing/ Bonuses:	Cash awards or additional compensation.
Retirement:	Employment offers or contributes to pension plan.

Your question about fringe benefits should stimulate the employer to talk about salary as well. If you don't get the information, however, follow up with a direct question about the salary range. You have the right to inquire, and you'd be crazy not to. How else will you know if the job is a real possibility for you?

Be careful about revealing too much. Put on a poker face when money is discussed, and never reveal your emotions. If the figure is incredibly low, watch what you say. After all, you're not obligated to accept the job. But if the salary is considerably more than you anticipated, don't overreact and don't reveal your amazement. If you can do the job, you're worth every cent.

Obviously, a display of greed would be inappropriate when you're talking about money, but there are two other attitudes that shouldn't be revealed either. Maybe the money isn't critical for you, but if you are flippant about money matters, the employer will give the job to someone who will appreciate it. If you appear indifferent, the job may well go to someone who cares.

The Bottom Line

Whether you sign a contract, receive a letter of appointment, or simply begin working on a verbal agreement depends on the type of employer and the kind of job.

Ted Nichols has just been hired. The employer has explained that his starting salary will be at the minimum end of the salary range, but his work will be reviewed after three months and, if satisfactory, an adjustment will be made. With no written agreement, Ted followed up this conversation with his own letter outlining the terms of the appointment.

421 8th Street
Casper, Wyoming 82001
March 25, 1989

Collette Gould, Vice President
Med Lab, Inc.
2000 Grand Avenue East
Salt Lake City, Utah 84108

Dear Ms. Gould:

I am pleased to accept the position of production supervisor offered to me on March 24, and I look forward to starting work on April 1.

As we discussed, it is my understanding that my work will be reviewed after three months and an adjustment in my salary will be considered.

I am excited about the opportunity to join your firm, and I look forward to working with you.

Sincerely,

Ted Nichols

Top Priority

For mid-level positions and for top executives, salaries and benefits can be the subject of extensive negotiations: proposals, counterproposals, compromises are all part of the game. Most job seekers, however, do not have these opportunities; salaries and wages are likely to be predetermined, though not necessarily set in stone, and there is little room for bargaining.

➡ Don't get so wrapped up in the salary issue that you forget about your primary goal: to find a job.

➡ If the salary isn't quite what you expected, remember that it is much easier to find a job when you are employed.

➡ Letting your pride get in the way can keep you from bringing home any kind of paycheck.

MONEY MATTERS

How much do I want? _____

What is the minimum dollar amount I can work for? _____

If an employer asks my salary range, what two figures will I use? (e.g. $15,000–$18,000; $30,000–$40,000)

_____ – _____ and _____ – _____

Do I know the average salary for comparable jobs? _____
(If no, ask around, check with your library, see what you can find out.)

My salary history is

JOB TITLE	STARTING SALARY	ENDING SALARY
_____	_____	_____
_____	_____	_____

Note: If you haven't worked in several years, respond by saying "not applicable."

Benefits most important to me are

1. _____   3. _____

2. _____   4. _____

AFTER THE INTERVIEW

The interview doesn't end when you walk out the door. You still have some things to do. Unless you were offered the job during the interview, this is not the time to celebrate. It is the time to think about what happened and to make a few notes for yourself.

To keep your facts and figures straight, use a file card or a page in a job notebook to record some basic facts and impressions.

JOB NOTEBOOK

Instant Replay

You'll probably never leave any interview perfectly satisfied with your performance. It's always possible to think of a more sophisticated response, a different answer, a smoother exit. Hindsight is always better, but you can't back up and go through the whole process again. The best you can do is to take a quick look at what happened so that you can make your next interview a little sharper, a little better.

Start by thinking about something that went well. Maybe you answered a difficult question in a way that even surprised you. Maybe the best thing was just that you were on time. But something good happened.

Don't ignore areas that didn't go so well, but don't dwell on them, either. If you had trouble with some of your responses, figure out some answers so that you'll be ready for them next time. If you think you talked too much, resolve to eliminate the fluff. If you think you were too passive, figure out how you can show your real enthusiasm. Did you try to be entertaining rather than informative? Plan to switch it around.

Your review of the interview should help you to improve where you can, but don't let it keep you from getting on with your job search. Use your energy to pursue other jobs, not to replay old interviews in slow motion.

Peering into the future probably won't get you very far, either. You don't have the information you need in order to make an accurate prediction of success or failure, and the outcome is really out of your hands, anyway. The only thing you should be worried about is whether you would accept the job if it's offered.

DON'T FORGET

You haven't finished your interview until you have sent a follow-up letter. It gives you one more chance to make a good impression. Most of your competition won't take the time to send one. Give yourself the advantage.

MAKE IT HAPPEN

Jobs go to those who want them, those who have put their acts together, those who have made all the pieces fit, those who have done the best jobs of promoting themselves.

▲ It doesn't matter how many candles blaze on your birthday cake;

▲ it doesn't matter if you look like Scarlett O'Hara or like Ma Kettle;

▲ it doesn't matter if your previous experiences have been glamorous or grimy;

▲ it doesn't matter if you've made your executive decisions in the kitchen or the boardroom;

▲ and it doesn't even matter if you sometimes feel like an adding machine in a computer world,

You Can Compete And You Can Be Hired.

Just because you're part of the "Over 40" crowd doesn't mean you have to settle for being unemployed, underemployed, or unhappily employed. Employers are waking up to the fact that your generation is going to be very much a part of the future. Your skills, your maturity, and your experiences are needed in today's workplace.

INDEX

ABOUT THE AUTHORS

Rebecca Jespersen Anthony and Gerald Roe are career specialists in the Educational Placement Office at The University of Iowa. They are coauthors of *How to Look Good to an Employer, Finding a Job in Your Field, Educators' Passport to International Jobs,* and *From Contact to Contract: A Teacher's Employment Guide.*